AUDUBON NATURE YEARBOOK 1990

1990 AUDUBON NATURE

FOG-FILLED VALLEYS IN THE NORTH CASCADES RANGE BY ART WOLFE

YEARBOOK

LES LINE, EDITOR

 Grolier Books, Danbury, Connecticut

Published by

Grolier Book Clubs Inc.
Grolier Inc.
Sherman Turnpike
Danbury, CT 06816

Book design by Nai Chang
Typography by Rochester Mono/Headliners

ISBN 1-55654-055-8
ISSN 0891-981X

Manufactured in the United States of America

CONTENTS

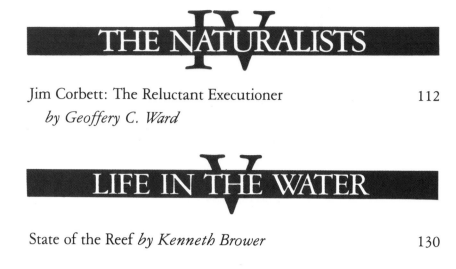

THE NATURALISTS IV

LIFE IN THE WATER V

WILD PLANTS AND MAN VI

SPECIAL PLACES VII

PREFACE

Nosing your Detroit-made steel-and-plastic wagon onto the westbound lanes of Interstate 80 at Omaha, Nebraska, and covering 600 miles a day (with an eye cocked for radar patrols), you can reach Sacramento in three days, easy. Nudging your ox-drawn homemade canvas-and-wood wagon onto the westbound lanes of the Great Platte River Road 140 years ago, covering 15 miles on a good day (with an eye cocked for Indians), you could reach California's gold-mining precincts in four and a half months, hard. Still, despite dangers and privations unknown in this coddled society, one wishes for an H.G. Wells time-machine that would enable a visit to an emigrant train, if only for a glimpse of a fabled prairie river, its environs, and its wildlife in their pristine glory.

Like I–80, the Great Platte River Road was a divided highway, with the river as its median. (The traffic, of course, was mostly one-way!) On the north side of the broad valley, pioneers out of Council Bluffs and Omaha followed the so-called Mormon Trail; on the south side, wagons launched from Independence or St. Joseph traversed the so-called Oregon Trail. On occasion, emigrants would catch a glimpse of their fellow travelers' campfires or sunlit wagontops across the wide river.

And wide it truly was. It resembled, wrote Oregon Trail historian Merrill Mattes, "no river any of the emigrants had ever seen before. It was miles wide and inches deep; thanks to Indian-set prairie fires and grazing buffalo, no timber grew on its banks.... Equally remarkable was the gelatinous character of the water itself." Noted one emigrant in his journal, "The water is so completely filled with glittering particles of micah or isinglass that its shining waves look to be rich with floating gold."

And the buffalo. Amazed another diarist, "We suddenly came upon an immense herd of these monsters of the Plains. They started to run in three mighty streams, two of which went directly through the gaps of our trains. As they thundered past in blind fear, shaking the ground beneath their feet, it seemed to me as though everything must be dashed to pieces."

Buffalo, of course, no longer thunder over the bluffs above the Platte, where corn long ago replaced the native prairie grasses. Plows and highways have obliterated most traces of the Oregon Trail except for the deepest hillside ruts. There are no copper-skinned nomads to drive nonexistent game with their fires, and so the banks of the Platte are now hidden by trees. And the river itself, its Rocky Mountain meltwaters dammed and diverted for thirsty cities and thirsty crops, its course shrunken and choked with cottonwood and willow, is but a shadow of its greatness.

Still, for all the changes that have occurred since the last wagon train passed this way shortly after the Civil War, the Platte River is the scene of one of the world's most fabulous wildlife spectacles. It is a show, however, that was never seen by emigrants. For their wagons left the Missouri River settlements too late to reach Grand Island on the Platte while the sandhill cranes were in congregation.

One wonders how the eloquent diarists among the 350,000 human migrants who embarked on the 2,400-mile overland trek to Oregon or California would have described this awesome gathering of avian migrants. A half-million vociferous cranes, birds nearly 4 feet tall with 6½-foot wingspans, assembled on the sandbars and wet meadows of the Platte for a month each spring, choosing mates in elaborate dances, and fattening up for the rigors of the nesting season on the marshy tundra of northern Canada, Alaska, and Siberia.

None, we suspect, could have written as moving an evocation as Paul Gruchow, whose essay on "The Ancient Faith of Cranes," accompanied by Ron Spomer's stunning photographs, is a highlight of this fourth edition of the *Audubon Nature Yearbook*. Come with Gruchow to his hiding place near the Platte on a March dawn:

"The morning had come while I was unawares. I stood, stretched my legs, shook the kinks out of my back. The thousands of cranes in the meadow shrieked in alarm and rose into the air as one body, the force of their wings sounding against the weight of the air like the rolling of a thousand snare drums. They fanned out until they filled the sky and churned forward, their wings wheezing, parting in a circle around me. I stood agape, like the women at the empty tomb.

7

When no sound remained but the champagne music of the redwings, I went to breakfast."

For millennia, the faith of the cranes—the faith that on the Platte they will find barren islands of sand on which to roost at night, safe from predators; and wet meadows on which to prance and feast—has been rewarded. But 70 percent of the Platte's historic flow has been claimed by man. No longer do surges of snowmelt from the mountains scour the bars of trees and brush; conservationists' chainsaws and bulldozers do the work of spring floods. And the avarice of boomtowners and irrigators would claim what little water still reaches the Great Bend in Nebraska. A dam called Two Forks on the South Platte in Colorado, one of several projects in blueprints, would store water to grow green lawns in the desert suburbs of Denver.

The first emigrants on the Oregon Trail, in 1840, followed tracks known only to fur-trapping mountainmen. The railroad pursued the last wagons, and the pavement of the Interstate was laid over their fading ruts. For less than two centuries, then, two great migrations have intersected on the Platte. But birds and men, in the words of Paul Gruchow, "have been moving not only in counterdirections but also at cross-purposes . . . The flyways of the cranes are the paths of nomads. Our highways are the routes of settlement, or more precisely, of occupation."

Whether our occupation of the Platte's environs will exclude cranes is the question of the moment.

Unlike most of the photographs found in these collections of *Audubon*'s best, Ron Spomer's memorable pictures of sandhill cranes were made on assignment. For much of a year—for a special issue on the Platte, its history, its treasures, and its troubles—the Nebraska native traveled the length of the river with camera in hand. He traveled three rivers, actually, for the main stem of the Platte is formed by two widely separated sibling streams, the North Platte and South Platte, that are born on the Continental Divide.

More often, as with Tom Ulrich's striking portrait of the predatory songbird known as the loggerhead shrike or "Butcherbird," Chuck Dressner's beautiful images of "Lilies of the Rainbow," or Larry West's revealing closeups of "The Humble Moss," the pictures were chosen from tens of thousands of transparencies submitted for our review by photographers the world over. Many of them come from hopeful amateurs, but frequently the best are the work of professionals. West is one of America's best-known nature photographers, and small things—mosses certainly qualify—are the favorite subjects for his lenses. Dwight Kuhn was a science teacher before turning to a freelance career, and there is no one better at insect photography, as witness his shots of life in a patch of milkweed, that "Underachiever of the Plant World." Dressner's specialty is industrial, commercial, and fashion photography, but he is often lured afield by the call of the wild. Or in this case the water lily ponds of the Missouri Botanical Garden.

Other times a call will go out from our picture department for images to fit a particular theme. An even dozen photographers are represented in our portfolio and article on fog, "The Stuff of Dreams and Dread." Meantime, the great effort that great nature photographs often demand is represented by Thomas Rountree's stunningly intimate portraits of shorebirds taken on San Francisco Bay's vanishing tidelands. Rountree, an environmental specialist for the Santa Clara County Transportation Agency, told me his secret: "I look for areas in the marsh, slough, or salt pond where there is a two- to four-foot dropoff adjacent to shallows only a few inches deep. Then I can conceal myself under a portable floating blind, position the camera (and 600mm telephoto lens) a few inches above the water, and shoot waterbirds at their eye level."

Sometimes, however, photographs to illustrate an *Audubon* story simply don't exist, and paintings are the answer. Arthur Singer, who has logged many visits to the forests and swamps of Trinidad, naturally got the call for our feature on "Asa Wright and Her Tropical Forest Ark." Born in New York City, Singer spent countless boyhood hours at the Bronx Zoo, sketching exotic birds. Schooled at Cooper Union, he turned from commercial art to nature in the early 1950s. With publication of the large-format book *Birds of the World* in 1961, followed by the best-selling Golden Guide *Birds of North America*, Singer jumped to the front rank of American bird painters. In 1982 he was commissioned by the U.S. Postal Service to create a sheet of fifty stamps showing the official birds of each state. One can say without fear of contradiction that Singer's paintings, like those of our magazine's namesake, have inspired countless thousands into a love for birds.

Les Line

Les Line, Editor, *Audubon* Magazine

MOSTLY MAMMALS

THE OLDEST WRITING

TEXT BY JOHN MADSON • PHOTOGRAPH BY TOM MURPHY

Opposite: Shadows still meet where a meadow vole and a kestrel met and wrote their lives "...in endless manuscript" of snow.

Meadow voles, being voles, often make mistakes. Such as electing to leave a cozy snow-tunnel in Yellowstone's Lamar Valley for a stroll up on the surface—and a rendezvous with a hovering kestrel.

The results are clearly apparent on the blank page of new snow. Did the vole see the little falcon and turn sharply in an effort to escape, managing a half-dozen more jumps before being struck? The sign doesn't say. But it does tell us that the kestrel struck true, shifted to secure its grip, and flew away with talons locked into breakfast. In the oldest of all writing, a Wyoming kestrel had added a new line to the ancient record.

Such writing can be read on wet sand, or mud that has just begun to firm, but is most legible on snow. Not because the tracks themselves are more clearly cut, for they may not be, but because they often tell more. The time of their making can be closely estimated. Delicate crystals at the edges of disturbed snow change quickly under sun and wind—their fragile latticework breaks and blurs and loses its fineness. Then, too, snow is a broad page that records tracks and trails over a great area while sand and mud may be limited to marginal notes.

Snow can reveal some strange goings-on.

I once started a fine white-tailed buck in a snowy timber and took up his trail. After he had bounded out of sight he began walking, skulking and pausing as his tribe often does. He left a classic trail in the light snow, his hooves showing the drag marks that allegedly always indicate big bucks. Coming to a barbed-wire fence that he could have leaped over from a standing start, he chose to crawl under it. I'll never understand how, or why, he maneuvered that massive, ten-point rack under a strand of wire only seventeen inches above the ground. But the snow sign was plain.

The daily doings of mice, voles, and other chisel-teeth aren't very gripping, but sooner or later their careers coincide with those of the wild hunters and things really pick up.

The red fox, in particular, writes adventures in snow that read like a paperback thriller. But while Reynard does well with the voles and mice that make up much of his diet, he doesn't always score on bigger game. I once trailed a red fox as he worked through a creekbottom weedpatch. His wandering tracks suddenly showed the intense focus of a hungry fox scenting food. There were the marks of his belly and luxuriant brush as he crept up on a big ring-necked pheasant roosting at the edge of the covert, and the fox had pounced just as the bird flushed. There was a scrambling, a desperate leap high into the air with ten feet of unmarked snow between takeoff point and landing, and one broken, thirty-inch tail feather. A very close thing. The fox had put on a short burst for several yards, coming to a skidding stop where he stood and watched his supper vanish, cackling in derision, over the winter skyline. Win some, lose some. I was only a witness after the fact, but it beat anything I saw that winter on TV.

Tragedy, comedy, drama, the ancient stories of survival and natural selection, all inscribed on a palimpsest of ice crystals and, like any fine reading, worth seeking out. No one admired it more than Ernest Thompson Seton, who versified:

Blest with a Magic Power is he,
Drinks deep where others sipped;
And Wild Things write their lives for him
In endless manuscript.

10

THE BEAVER IS ONE SMART RAT

TEXT BY HOPE RYDEN · PHOTOGRAPHY BY WAYNE LANKINEN

"...who would have
thought a rodent capable
of so much charm?"

The beaver I had named Lily heaved herself out of the pond, lumbered up the bank to where I was seated, and, cocking her head, viewed me out of one eye. I spoke softly to her and took care not to make any sudden moves. When Lily had seen all she wanted, she turned, waddled downhill, and slipped noiselessly into the water.

Had I passed muster? Evidently so, for after that the six animals I had been watching for several weeks came ashore from time to time and fed on vegetation just a few feet from where I stationed myself each night.

I had obtained a permit to make after-hours observations of *Castor canadensis* in New York's Harriman State Park, a 47,000-acre, heavily wooded tract normally closed to visitors after dark. It was an ideal place to make a study, for trapping is not allowed here. Moreover, it is just a ten-minute drive from my house in the Ramapo Mountains, thus allowing me to turn night into day and fall into bed at dawn, shortly after my nocturnal subjects retired into their big, conical stick lodge.

There were six animals in my colony. Lily, the matriarch, was the second largest beaver in this family, and her long, narrow snout and a touch of gray around her nose pad made her easily identifiable.

Her mate, the Inspector General, was the only other full-grown beaver on the pond. He might as easily have been recognized by his behavior, which reflected an almost obsessive concern with the condition of the dam. Every evening, upon leaving the lodge, he made a beeline for this five-foot-high structure and cruised its fifty-yard length searching for leaks. Whenever he discovered a problem, he would immediately stop paddling and, aiming his nose at the trouble spot, idle for a minute or two as if contemplating what to do. Quickly I would set up my camera, hoping to catch some action before the fast-fading light was entirely gone. But the Inspector General was never in a hurry to make repairs, and inevitably he would paddle away and feed on water lily pads for a couple of hours before returning with repair material in tow.

This delayed response challenged my preconceived idea that planning and forethought play no part in beaver dam construction. Like most beaver-watchers I was familiar with the work of the Swedish biologist Lars Wilsson, who demonstrated that captive beavers build dams haphazardly in response to recordings of running water. From this experiment I had leaped to the conclusion that the animal is programed to silence the gurgle of a stream. In a year and a half of intensive beaver-watching, however, I was forced to reexamine this idea. Although my beavers were often alerted to breaks in their dam by water noise, more often than not they ignored this signal and made no repairs—especially when water levels in their pond were sufficient to meet their needs. Moreover, in winter they created a spillway over their dam that loudly siphoned off water and lowered the level of the pond. This created an air space between the water surface and the roof of ice that covered their world.

The remaining four members of what I came to call the Lotus-Eaters Colony consisted of two yearlings and two kits. The two yearlings I named Laurel and the Skipper.

Easygoing Laurel seemed unafraid of me. She was an astonishing color—bright auburn. Frequently she was accompanied by one or the other of the kits, whom I named Lotus and Blossom. These youngsters were indistinguishable during their first months but as yearlings were easy to differentiate by color.

I had not imagined that beavers would be so charming. After all, *Castor canadensis* is a rodent, a type of animal not generally looked upon with favor. But the beaver, I soon realized, is as far removed from a mouse or a lemming as the lemur, a fellow primate, is from me. Swiss biologist Georg Pilleri recently analyzed the beaver's brain and pro-

nounced its cortex to be far more developed than that of any other member of the order Rodentia. To this fact he credits the beaver's ability to adapt to vastly different situations.

At an international beaver symposium held in Helsinki in 1982, French biologist P. Richard reported on behavioral tests he conducted that support Pilleri's view of the beaver's intelligence. In one test he presented a piece of bread suspended by a string to a muskrat, a rat, and a beaver. The muskrat and the rat (often cited as an intelligent animal) jumped at the bait and attempted to tear and snatch pieces from it (sort of like bobbing for apples). The beaver studied the situation, then cut the string. (I am re-

"This genial rodent, I soon realized, is as far removed from a mouse or lemming as the lemur, a fellow primate, is from me."

15

minded of how the Inspector General studied any break in his dam for a minute or two.)

In another of Richard's tests a beaver solved the problem of how to fell a willow tree that was protected at the base with a wire net. The animal stacked refuse beside the tree, then climbed on this platform and made a cut above the wire. This capacity for adaptation, which is sometimes called the "behavior of detour," is well known in the chimpanzee but has been overlooked in the beaver.

It is in its social development that the beaver most distinguishes itself from others in its order. There is little time or need in the short life spans of mice or lemmings to develop complex social relationships. These animals produce large numbers of fast-maturing young who are out of the nest in days, breeding in weeks, and dead by age two. By contrast, the beaver is long-lived and a slow breeder, producing but a single litter annually, usually only two or three kits. These young remain at home until they are nearly two years old and sometimes much longer. During this dependency, they have time to perfect their behavioral repertoire, especially construction activities.

A beaver colony therefore consists of the breeding pair (monogamous while both of the partners live), their yearling young of the previous year, their kits of the year, and any older offspring who, having failed to find suitable habitat in which to settle, return home. These already mature beavers are accepted back into the family fold, sometimes after an absence of several years. Unrelated beavers who trespass on a colony's claim are warned to leave by the colony's many scent mounds.

To maintain such long-lasting family ties, the beaver has evolved social techniques to defuse hostility and promote peaceful relations. Yet to the casual observer this fact may not be readily apparent. Beavers emerge from their lodge in the evening, and for the first hour or so their single-minded aim is to feed. This often solo activity normally lasts until dark. Even when working on a communal project, beavers tend to act independently and appear to ignore one another.

Inside a beaver lodge, however, intimate contact is unavoidable. This is especially true during the cold months, when the animals are confined in tight quarters for weeks on end. There is no escaping relatives. Beavers do not hibernate.

Since all the lodge's exit holes are underwater, once the pond has frozen over, a beaver does not see the sky or climb onto land until a good thaw. To eat, it must exit through one of two or three plunge holes and swim under a roof of ice to the family food larder—a pile of branches that the beavers assiduously gathered and submerged in front of the lodge in late fall.

Oversized lungs and liver notwithstanding, a beaver cannot hold its breath indefinitely. After twenty minutes underwater, it will need to return to the lodge and inhale oxygen that leaks into its dwelling through a vent at the top. Still, within this time a beaver can debark a thick bough (the wood holds no nutritional value for it) and can perhaps dig up a water-lily tuber from the floor of the pond as well.

Beavers are well adapted for underwater living. Whenever they dive, transparent membranes slide over their eyes and protect them. Their valvular ears and nostrils can be closed at will. And underwater dining poses no problem; their loose cheeks can be sucked closed behind their big orange front teeth, permitting them to chip away at bark without gagging on water.

More often than not, however, a beaver will simply clip a branch from the food store and return with it to the lodge, where, in a small antechamber at the top of one of the plunge holes, it can breathe, eat, and drain. After climbing higher into the main quarters, it must nose about in the dark to reclaim space amid a mass of damp beavers.

Rats become vicious when crowded, and humans suffer "cabin fever" when locked with one another over long stretches. How do beavers maintain peaceful relations while confined?

To gain insight into this question Canadian experimenter Françoise Patenaude cut a window in the back of a beaver lodge through which she watched a family of beavers over a two-year period. She saw little aggression. On the contrary, the animals got along well, even slept together in a friendly heap, sometimes clinging to one another. When awake they spent much time grooming each other's fur, a pacifying activity (also an essential one if the animals are to remain waterproof). When a dispute did arise over a branch or over space, the problem was quickly resolved with a growl, shove, or stare.

Yet even such a socially adapted animal as the beaver is capable of aggression. Beaver fights, while rare, are savage, often resulting in the death of one of the combatants. Likely these battles are fought over territory.

To avoid such dangerous clashes, beavers mark their territories with "no trespassing" signs—mounds of mud and leaves—around their ponds and along their travel routes. Each builder then sprays this debris with scent from two pairs of glands inside its cloaca, a kind of pouch that also contains the animal's anus, urethra, and sex organs. Spray from the anal glands may communicate information about the animal's age, sex, health, and diet; spray from the castor glands may be a kind of fixative that preserves these messages for all strange beavers to "read."

In April, shortly after ice-out releases beavers from their winter confinement, scent-marking activity peaks. This is when the new two-year-olds leave their parental ponds to seek territories of their own. Freshly made scent notices no doubt warn the émigrés to pass through already occupied water. Conversely, the mounds may also inform some wanderers where a vacancy exists. For example, when either member of a mated pair dies, the absence of its scent throughout an occupied area may invite a two-year-old of the same sex to move in.

After April, mound-making activity declines, although I observed a resurgence of it in July on the part of the male I called the Skipper. For a time I had lost track of him. Upon nearing his second birthday he had left home, accompanied by his sister, Laurel—the distinctive auburn-colored beaver. Although I searched the watershed, I could find no sign of them. Then I discovered the pair homesteading together on quite another stream. They had moved overland, crossing a busy road, to find this site. I was overjoyed to witness their transformation of a meadow into a beaver pond, providing habitat for herons, ducks, and frogs. This was a dynamic example of the cyclical character of the beaver's role in nature, for the meadow itself had evolved from an ancient beaver pond.

Then the female began to make regular visits to her former home, perhaps to help care for the two new kits born to her mother. En route between the two watersheds, she was killed by a car.

I don't know how or even if the Skipper became aware that he was now going it alone; but shortly after Laurel's death, he ceased all labor on the new dam, and it fell into disrepair. At the same time, however, he began erecting the biggest scent mounds I had seen anywhere—huge piles of mud and leaf debris. Was he advertising for a companion? Possibly, for within a month a small beaver joined him and construction resumed on the waterworks.

A beaver's dexterity is comparable to that of many primates and is far superior to that

Beaver kits in a lodge. "Until kits are about a month old they are confined to the lodge, where they are waited on by all members of the family. They are never left unattended."

of all members of its own order, Rodentia. Yet, like human babies, kits must acquire manual skill through trial and error, practice, and observation of others. All my adult beavers deftly rolled lily pads into manageable cigar shapes before inserting them into their mouths. Some even made double rolls. At five months, however, the kits had not yet acquired this trick. They gripped the big, floppy leaves awkwardly, tried to eat around the edges, and sometimes ended up wearing them on their heads. Yet in time, possibly as an outgrowth of frequently feeding with adults, they too began to roll the pads.

The debate over what behavior a beaver learns and what is coded into its genes is a subject for a full-length book. Clearly some elements of dam and lodge construction are innate. For example, beavers go through building motions at an early age and out of context. At the same time, the animal's unusually long dependency argues that learning must also play a significant role in organizing and perfecting this inborn behavior. Like the young of wild felids, which instinctively know how to stalk and pounce on imaginary prey but do not automatically know how to hunt and kill food, young beavers may need to observe older animals at work to put their instinctive movements to effective use. In fact, kits do not

work on dams and lodges during their first year, though they sometimes make digging and building motions in thin air.

Several researchers contend that beavers less than a year old do not help put in the winter food store either. I found otherwise. My late-born 1984 beaver babies took part in this work when only three months old, albeit incompetently at first. Quite by accident I created an opportunity to witness the kits in food-storing behavior.

For several nights I had observed Lily and the Inspector General cutting, towing, and sinking high-bush blueberry and barberry in the water in front of their freshly plastered lodge, situated on the far bank from my viewing station. It occurred to me that I ought to bring some better beaver fare for them to store. The next night I delivered a bundle of aspen branches, a favorite food that did not grow around their pond.

The beavers' response was to stop work on the winter food larder and feed. The following night, however, Lily began storing my offering. While her still-infantile kits complained, she made trip after trip to the lodge, towing branches at a furious pace. In her hurry she sometimes gathered two or even three boughs in her mouth before departing. On her return trip she snatched water lily pads and ate on the run.

HOPE RYDEN

Over the next few nights the Inspector General and the two yearlings also participated in this effort. And by the following week one of the two kits had joined the work force. Awkwardly gripping an aspen bough by the middle, he attempted to push it in front of him as he headed in the general direction of the lodge. Water resistance created by the wrongly held branch caused the little beaver to swim in zig-zags. Even so, he managed to move the branch across the pond to the lodge, then dove and planted it in the growing food raft.

The next night I watched again as this youngster struggled with a recalcitrant aspen bough. And again he attempted to shove it across the pond. This time, however, he happened to follow in his mother's wake and may well have observed the proper method by which to transport branches. For suddenly he stopped and transferred his grip from the middle to the butt of the bough, whereupon it drifted to his side and could easily be towed. Whether this kit learned the trick through trial and error or by imitating his mother is not important. The fact is he had to learn *how* to tow, even though the impulse to do so had likely been encoded.

I dreaded seeing my beavers sequester themselves for winter, and I got the impression that they were in no hurry to be locked under the ice either. When the pond froze over, they systematically shattered the newly formed ice by bumping it from below. Once they had created a hole, they would surface and push down on the edges of the opening from above, using their hands to break off slabs.

The sound of this work, which they carried on all night, reverberated like the ringing of metal on metal. After I satisfied myself that the weird noise was indeed being created by beavers bumping ice from below, I marveled at the behavior. I had never read reports of it. Was it unique to this colony? Later in the month I looked in on one of the colonies of beavers I was keeping tabs on in Massachusetts and found that they, too, were hard at work keeping open a last swimming channel in their all but frozen-over pond.

As the weather grew colder the beavers stopped battling ice and retired into their lodge. I was sorry to see them go. Several times during winter I visited the dwelling, which was covered with snow and looked like an igloo. Occasionally from deep within, I heard the murmur of beavers and was reassured that at least some of them were surviving the season.

When a small circle of ice melted directly above their food raft, probably as a result of so much feeding activity, I sat by this open-

The author's subjects— at left, Lily, the Inspector General at right, and one of their kits—feeding on aspen branches in their home pond at Harrison State Park. "Several researchers contend that beavers less than a year old do not help put in the winter food store. I found otherwise."

19

ing and waited for a sign of life. One afternoon, just as the wintry light began to fail, the Inspector General rose out of the water and heaved himself onto an exposed rock. Soon the two kits emerged, and after taking a few turns around the small swimming hole, they began increasing its dimensions by breaking ice along its edges. Then they vanished. A few minutes later the Inspector General climbed up on the dam, having swum under the ice for some one hundred yards. The beavers were as ready as the willow trees to burst forth in spring.

By then it was late February, when beavers mate. Copulation would take place in the cold water, belly to belly. As a prelude to this act, courting behavior had been going on for some time. As early as October I had seen Lily and the Inspector General climb onto the bank and rub their faces together while emitting cooing noises. Lars Wilsson (a strict determinist who can hardly be accused of having an anthropomorphic perspective), described the behavior of a courting beaver couple as follows:

"They sleep curled up close together during the daytime, and at night they seek each other out at regular intervals to groom one another or just simply to sit close side by side and 'talk' for a little while in special contact sounds, the tones and nuances of which seem to a human expressive of nothing but intimacy and affection."

About one hundred days after Lily and the Inspector General mated, two kits were born. One, a blonde, I named Buttercup. But I was not to see this infant or its brown sibling, Huckleberry, for several weeks. Until kits are about a month old they are confined to the lodge, where they are waited on by all members of the family. They are, in fact, never left unattended. One baby-sitter always remains with them while the others feed.

The young are open-eyed at birth and capable of swimming at four days old. One would think such precocial babies would not require as much overseeing as they get. But the buoyant kits are incapable of diving, and should they escape the lodge, they would not be able to return by the only route available —the underwater hole.

So they are guarded and waited on. If a rambunctious infant falls into an exit hole, one of the ever-attentive adults or yearlings is ready to haul it to safety. The kit will be seized by its tail and nosed up to the antechamber, or the adult will lift it, hold it between forepaws and chin, and walk bipedally, carrying it to the living quarters. This second method of transporting young, incidentally, is not seen in the European beaver, *Castor fiber.*

I was, of course, on hand for the debut of the kits when they were about five weeks old. At first one or more watchful adults swam alongside them in case a piggyback ride was necessary. But I always had difficulty seeing these young ones. They emerged when the light was all but gone. And I resisted the temptation to thrash my way around the pond for a closer look, for I was determined not to allow these new kits to become habituated to me.

By this time I had discouraged the older beavers from approaching me: I fear for the safety of any wild animal that puts its trust in humans. So one evening I had brought a large shovel to the pond, and every time one of the beavers swam near me I raised this "tail" and slapped the water with it to signal "danger" in beaver language.

My bizarre behavior elicited quite different responses from the various-age cohorts. The adult pair reacted by hissing and swimming rapidly about. At one point they even seemed to make an effort to corral their offspring, who were just shy of yearling status, and move them away from shore. The youngsters, on the other hand, approached even closer to where I stood on the dam, and whenever I brought down the shovel, they whacked the water with their tails. Were these two juveniles playing a game with me? And what could I make of the parents' seeming attempts to herd them away? I could find no description literature of one beaver approaching a threat to protect another.

So many intriguing questions remained unanswered—questions I wouldn't have thought to ask before I began observing *Castor canadensis.* I had known in advance that I would be impressed by my subjects' engineering feats—their dam-building, pond-making, house-raising, canal-dredging, and tree-felling. I had even anticipated my own delight in seeing the array of birds and animals that the beaver's tireless efforts to conserve water inevitably attracts to the ponds— ducks and grebes and birds of prey, otters and deer and muskrat, turtles and fish and frogs. What I had not expected was that the beaver would prove to be so genial and appealing. But then who would have thought a rodent capable of so much charm?

ARMADILLOS MAKE ME SMILE A LOT

TEXT BY DONALD G. SCHUELER • PHOTOGRAPHY BY JEFF FOOTT

Unafraid of man, it grunts, it swims, it eats ants. Why does fame elude the armadillo?

It has been almost twenty years since I met my first nine-banded armadillo, but I still remember the occasion clearly. I was out for a stroll on some land I had just bought in southwestern Mississippi when the evening quiet was interrupted by the blundering advance of an unseen something in a nearby tangle of yaupon and gallberry. I guessed it was a half-wild woods hog. What emerged seconds later was the oddest looking little animal I had ever seen. It hustled out of the thicket with a preoccupied, fuddy-duddy air and headed straight for me, totally oblivious of my presence until I moved my foot from under its snuffling nose. At that, it let out a flustered *Gurk!* and scuttled off. But only a few yards away it came to a halt. Then, apparently deciding that I was more than its tiny intellect could deal with, it began rooting for grubs in the leafy earth.

If Lewis Carroll's aardvark had emerged through the looking glass, I could hardly have been more surprised. Or amused. I had seen pictures of armadillos before, but these had not prepared me for the sheer goofiness, the thrown-togetherness, of the real article. Even as the usual comparisons occurred to me—piglet snout, jackass ears, football physique, turtle tail—I realized that the art of analogy was not meant to cope with this animal. It looked like itself and nothing else.

Given its appearance and general bearing, I wondered why such a droll creature had not become a folkloric star, right up there with Br'er Rabbit and Woody Woodpecker. I could understand how Uncle Remus had missed out, since in his day armadillos had barely settled in this country. But what was Walt Disney's excuse? And why, in more recent years, had no armadillo been cast for a leading role in "Pogo"?

In the larger world of popular culture, fame still eludes the armadillo. Only in Texas, its original home base in this country, has it achieved a certain celebrity. Lone Star historians have recognized the animal's good sense in arriving at just about the time Texas joined the Union. Lone Star legislators, noticing that some armadillo traits "parallel the attributes that distinguish a true Texan," have twice nominated it as the state mammal. For a time during the seventies, a Lone Star brewing company advertised its notoriously insatiable thirst for Lone Star Beer. Also during the seventies, the Armadillo World Headquarters, Austin's famed center for country and rock music, adopted it as the unofficial mascot of Lone Star hippies. More recently, Lone Star boosters have renamed it the Texas Panda and shipped it off to the Peking Zoo. And, in an inspired moment, one Lone Star artist immortalized its nearsighted attempt to mate with the armadillo-shaped dome of the state capitol.

But even Texas-sized whimsy has a hard time outdoing the armadillo's reality. To begin with, it belongs to a very ancient order of animals, the Edentata, whose other modern representatives are the various sloths and anteaters—every one of them peculiar-looking. The armadillo family, the Dasypodidae, includes about twenty present-day species, all confined to Central and South America; the one exception is our nine-banded variety, otherwise known as *Dasypus novemcinctus,* named for the number of leathery bands that girdle its shapeless waist. It is the most widespread and generally successful of its clan. This may be because it has a talent for evolutionary compromise. At a maximum fourteen pounds, it can't compare in size with the 130-pound giant armadillo of eastern South America; but it is nothing like as fragile as the endangered pink fairy armadillo of southern South America, which wears a little cap and cape of pink armor over an otherwise hairy body. It isn't able to roll up inside its shell like the three-banded armadillo, but it can curl up enough to partly shield its tender underparts from bullying dogs. And although it cannot hibernate in winter as the Patagonian pygmy armadillo is said to do, it can bear up under much colder temperatures than scientists once thought.

With its middle-of-the-road approach to life, the nine-banded armadillo has been able to adapt to a wider range of habitats than any of the other Dasypodidae and has

to Attila the Hun. Not that they accomplished this feat without considerable help from us.

Especially in the western part of its range, changes in agricultural practices increased the armadillo's insect food supply. In the South, the spread of the armadillo occurred in part because dealers shipped many of the animals off to roadside exhibits from which they promptly escaped, and jokesters shipped others to nonplussed friends who promptly turned them loose. One way or another, they were showing up in Louisiana and Arkansas by 1920. During the same decade, escapees from zoos began the conquest of Florida—an undertaking only recently completed when animals migrating west through the Panhandle met, in what must have been a red-letter day for armadillos, with others migrating east from Alabama. In the 1940s the first armadillos started showing up in southern Mississippi. By the sixties they had begun their march through Georgia. Even now, the enterprising little beasts have not called it quits. Though colder latitudes have slowed them down, they are presently occupying South Carolina in the East and, to everyone's surprise, crossing the border into wintry Missouri in the West.

The armadillo's reproductive habits are said to have helped it on its way, though why, I don't know. Compared with most smallish mammals, it isn't all that prolific. However, like everything else about the animal, its sex life is a bit eccentric. In contrast to other quadrupeds, it assumes the missionary position when mating. Once impregnated, the female may postpone gestation for months if she feels like it. Even more outlandishly, four embryos—never more or less—are conceived from the single fertilized ovum. Hence, the offspring are genetically identical quadruplets, all of the same sex.

It is no wonder that scientists in the fields of reproductive physiology and genetics take considerable interest in the animal. Even more important, it serves a crucial purpose in the study and control of Hansen's disease, or leprosy. Armadillos are peculiarly susceptible to contracting the disease under laboratory conditions; and because of their rather low body temperatures they make ideal hosts for its bacilli. Thus they provide scientists with a dependable reservoir of microorganisms for immunology research. There is the remote risk that a person can contract leprosy by handling infected animals.

Much of the armadillo's success as a colonist has to do with its unfussy eating habits. It is an accomplished digger with an insatiable appetite for insects—mostly harmful

long been at home in most of South and Central America. During the mid-19th Century it crossed the Rio Grande and established itself in Texas. For the next three quarters of a century it was content to limit its homesteading to the south and central sections of that state. But in the 1920s armadillos began to colonize other Gulf states with a swiftness that would have done credit

beetles and their grubs—as well as assorted centipedes, worms, spiders, slugs, and the occasional small amphibian or snake. The fire ant, an immigrant like the armadillo but a totally unwelcome one, is also on the menu. I am reminded of this fact whenever I walk through the piney woods at my place in Mississippi and note the plundered ant hills along the paths. Having been bitten ten thousand times by fire ants, I bless the armadillo's appetite even as I marvel at its imperviousness to pain. It is the only wildlife species in the southern forests thick-skinned (or masochistic) enough to tackle a nest of these ferocious little pests.

Besides relishing noxious beetles, termites, and fire ants, not to mention contracting leprosy on our behalf, armadillos have a virtue that especially recommends them to other wildlife species: They dig sizable burrows. The Deep South has no equivalent of the groundhog or badger, unless one counts the threatened gopher tortoise. So the armadillo's tunnels—anywhere from four to twelve feet long—have become important hideouts for other creatures in the hound-ridden, fire-swept southern woods. At one time or another I have seen an opossum, a black racer, a large, beautiful corn snake, and a rabbit ducking into apparently active burrows without any objection from the landlord. In the same tolerant spirit, armadillos often use each other's dens when they need a

place to hide. They are not gregarious, but they seem innocent of any territorial imperative above or below ground. Often I have watched two or three adults grubbing about within a few yards of each other, studiously minding their own business like pedestrians on a New York street. Despite their collective prowess as colonizers, individual animals like to stay put. An armadillo is considered well traveled if it covers a dozen acres in a lifetime.

Sad to say, the armadillo is not a clever animal. It steps out into traffic without looking right or left. Even when the wheels of an oncoming vehicle miss it, it jumps up and brains itself on the axle with dependable regularity. Even more fatally, it has not learned to be afraid of man. One can make excuses for it; its rooting habits, after all, require it to keep its head buried half the time. But above-ground it is just as unalert. Countless times, as at that first meeting years ago, armadillos have waddled up to me as if I were no more animate than a fencepost—even when I was being animate. On one occasion I stood on the bank of my pond directly above a half-grown youngster as it lolled on its back in the shallows, totally unaware of me. When I left several minutes later, having resisted the temptation to tickle its stomach, the armadillo was still wallowing about, happily waving its stumpy legs in the air and grunting like Porky Pig.

In part, the "conflict" between armadillos and man relates to our manicured lawns and tidy flowerbeds. Personally, I can't understand why anyone would prefer these to armadillos, but apparently many people do. Even granting that preference, however, an either/or choice should not be necessary in most cases. Damage done by the animal's unauthorized tilling is usually not serious and can be repaired easily—a matter of tamping dirt back into a few holes or pushing the mulch back around the azaleas. With a small investment of money and effort, even that bother can be avoided. Since armadillos never know where they are going until they get there, they usually can be pointed in a different direction by a barrier no higher than a foot-high wicket border.

Still, I concede, albeit sullenly, that property owners have the right to take the lethal way out in defending their boring rows of bean sprouts or garish tulips against some exceptionally persistent animal. But no such justification applies to that vast legion of gun-toting clods (several specimens of which lurk near my property) who shoot any armadillo they see, anywhere, anytime, for the same reason they shoot all sorts of other more-or-less unoffending wildlife: because they like to kill critters and any "lil' ole" excuse will do. To hear these fellows badmouth armadillos, you would suppose the animals live on quail eggs, dig holes in pastures just so cows will break their legs, and gobble up cantaloupes, watermelons, and other farm produce by the ton. In fact, research indicates that although an armadillo may sample a quail egg if it trips over one, its small mouth and minimal teeth are not designed for egg-eating. Or for devouring agricultural crops, peanuts occasionally excepted. As for broken-legged cattle, the armadillo's diagonal burrow has got to rank way below lightning, hunters' bullets, or, for that matter, vertical stump holes as a freak cause of livestock mishaps.

However, when these charges have been thrown out of court, the prosecution still has one witness left whose testimony can hardly be ignored. This is the late, great naturalist Archie Carr, who admitted in an article that he was disenchanted with armadillos, at least the ones he knew in central Florida. He blamed the animals for undermining the ecology of the leaf-mold stratum on the floor of Florida's hummock forests. It's bad enough that they deplete populations of interesting microbes, insects, spiders, toads, and snakes, but even worse, their continual rooting aerates the mold itself, aborting the

process whereby vegetable litter becomes rich organic soil.

It is not for the likes of me to challenge the likes of Archie Carr. No doubt armadillos are a problem in the specialized ecological setup of central Florida hummocks, although even there, as Dr. Carr conceded in passing, evidence suggests they may finally be getting more into balance with their environment. All I can say is that on my own tract of hardwood hollows and piney woods, which is as representative of armadillo country as any you can find in the Deep South, the harmful effects he describes are just not evident. True, I haven't censused the microbe and insect larvae populations in the hardwood bottoms, but the oft-rooted mulch seems to decay in no time at all. Indeed, organic gardeners assure me that regular turning helps the process along. As for the more visible small fauna such as skinks, daddy longlegs, snakes, and toads, they are happily in good supply, along with the armadillos themselves.

On that positive note, the defense will rest its case. It goes without saying that my verdict is already in. Armadillos may not be good for my flowerbeds, but they make me smile a lot. And I would hate to think of my Mississippi place without them. There, as well as in the more private landscape where my imagination builds legends to suit itself, Br'er Armadillo will always have top billing as a favorite comic hero.

The armadillo is a digger with an insatiable appetite for insects, like termites.

THE WOLF AT THE WINDOW

TEXT BY ELLEN HAWKINS

·

PAINTING BY JACK UNRUH

THUMP . . . THUMP . . . THUMP! Loud and insistent knocking shocked us out of our sleep. Who would come to our snowbound North Woods cabin in the middle of the night? Gary grabbed the flashlight and hurried into the kitchen. Then, realizing that the sound was not coming from the porch entry, he swung the beam toward the living room's ground-level windows. I caught up just as he froze in his tracks.

"My God, Ellen, it's the wolf!"

Stunned, we stared at the face pressed against the glass, at the blazing yellow eyes and broad cheek ruffs of an adult timber wolf.

This wolf was not a stranger to us. I had first seen him a week before, curled up by a deer carcass in a clearing at the base of our ridge.

During the coldest winter months the Minnesota Department of Natural Resources supplies us with road-killed deer for use as wildlife food. We pull the deer remains by toboggan to a clearing two hundred yards below and in full view of our house. It's a place where wild animals can feed and feel secure—a mile from the road, with Superior National Forest all around.

Blue jays, gray jays, ravens, foxes, fishers, martens, and weasels feed on the deer carcasses throughout the winter. In spring, to our delight, they are joined by bald eagles and turkey vultures.

Wolves stop here rarely, and we feel lucky to hear them howl or to find their tracks. Although this part of the state is their only stronghold in the nation, outside of Alaska, they are not common even here. Their numbers are stretched thin across thousands of acres of forest. This scarcity and their shy

nature mean that a glimpse of a timber wolf is a rare occurrence and that a chance to watch one is a special treat.

When I first spotted the wolf at the deer carcass I excitedly watched from the living room window and wrote in my journal as he awoke from his nap, licked his feet, and stood and stretched.

December 8: "The wolf is finally up, and I can see that he's quite dark, his guard hairs black-tipped gray, with lighter eyebrow spots and cheeks, and reddish fur behind the ears. His tawny legs seem spindly above those great big feet. And he has a radio collar! I didn't know there was anybody studying wolves in this part of the forest.

"A wolf does something magic to the place where he is. Here is the same familiar scene, the dark edge of the forest meeting the bright snow of the clearing, the big spruce in the foreground and the vertical lines of the young aspen thicket to the east. But now the wolf is here and there is a vital focus. The frozen scene is charged with life."

But my great excitement at having him here soon became subdued. I wrote:

"This is a hurt wolf. He holds up his right front foot and limps. A couple of times he has fallen in soft snow on raven runs between the old deer carcass at the edge of the woods and the fresh carcass in the clearing. His tail is tightly down, except when he's after the ravens, and then it's held out only slightly.

"His movements seem stiff and awkward. He's very thin. Standing, facing away from me, his body looks narrower than his head. And he doesn't seem enthused about things. He is droopy, indecisive, unhappy.

"When he first woke up he did some grooming, but otherwise he's been lying down, either tightly curled or watching those pesky ravens or looking around in a desultory way, ears drooped slightly back.

"The ravens are getting braver, and he can hardly stand seeing them at a deer. They come dropping down out of the trees around whichever deer he's not at, and he has to hurry over to get them up. They scatter briefly, but here they come again, settling down around the other deer, and back he has to go."

December 10: "The wolf is still at the deer. In fact, if he ever leaves it, it must be at night. He seems weaker and has long since conceded the older carcass to the ravens. Now his only means of defending the other is to lie on it. Even so, they come sidling closer, stand nonchalantly around for a while, then step up closer yet. The wolf curls his lips as he watches with his head on his paws. Suddenly the ravens scatter in a mad flapping of black

wings. The wolf must have snarled. But a minute later the birds are back.

"I watched as Gary went crunching down the snowshoe trail, out of sight but not out of hearing of the clearing. As he reached the bottom of the hill, the wolf stood up and watched alertly, ears focused, but a moment later he was relaxed and lying down again."

December 12: "This morning, the wolf's fifth day in the clearing, it seemed time to take him another deer. He didn't seem to have as much energy as he's had; there wasn't much vigor in the way he would shake and stretch. He had been spending most of his time lying down, and at times appeared to be coughing. Even if the old deer carcass had some meat left, it would surely be getting hard to reach.

"Until now, we'd tried to stay out of sight, wanting him to feel comfortable about staying with this easy food source. Now I stood in front of the house where he could see me, hoping that somehow he would be used to us. He must have had glimpses and smells of us over the past several days. But no. He got right up and hurried into the woods, looking back over his shoulder at me. I skidded the deer down and retreated, but he hasn't returned."

December 13: "The wolf is back. He's eaten a little, but has spent most of the day lying between the two carcasses at the center of the clearing. He makes no effort to fend off the ravens, and they are all over both deer."

Near sunset of that day he was gone. Ten hours later we were confronted by his face pressed against our window.

As we stood gaping, too astonished for the moment to do anything, we saw the wolf's nose once more thump hard against the glass before the face withdrew from the circle of light. We heard crunching steps in the snow at the corner of the house, then silence. Was he gone? We scraped a hole in the frost on the south window and again found ourselves trading stares with the wolf. The roof of our pit-style greenhouse is attached to the house just below the south window. The wolf had climbed a snowdrift onto the greenhouse and now sat leaning against the window and looking back over his shoulder at us.

Now came a flurry of activity: getting together chicken leftovers, gravy, butter, and hot water, slipping on our parkas, and hurrying out to see what the wolf wanted. Gary tossed the chicken onto the greenhouse roof and pushed the gravy pan up to him with a snow shovel. I stood behind Gary with the flashlight, the backup person. We didn't think a normal wolf would attack a person, but this wolf was doing something we had never heard of a wolf doing. We didn't know what to expect. The wolf just watched, looking alertly first at us, then at the food.

Now another flurry, this time of indecision. Was he hypothermic? Did he want to come in? Should he? How could we get him in, anyway? We certainly couldn't just leave him there, this wolf we had watched and been concerned about all week. On that still, moonless night, the temperature was twenty-five degrees below zero. Surely it would help to get him into a warmer place. Gary got a blanket, went along the edge of the greenhouse behind the wolf, and threw it across the animal's back. The wolf jumped, then settled down. We thought we might be able to catch him. So I went up to the shed to get the stove going, thinking that the shed might be the place for him, and Gary got the old green quilt.

By the time I got back to the house, Gary was coming around the corner carrying a blanket-draped bundle. He had thrown the quilt over the wolf and, getting no adverse reaction, had tucked it around the animal and pulled him across the slippery roof to the edge. He had looked under to see where the wolf was, covered him again, and scooped him up into his arms. The shed was forgotten. I opened the door, and Gary carried him inside. Beginning to lose his grip, he just made it to the living room and eased the wolf to the floor. He lifted the blanket and stepped back. The wolf looked around in a dazed kind of way. Twenty-five minutes after the knocks on the window he was inside.

Now what? First, get Tom. He is our good friend and neighbor, our only neighbor within twelve miles, and we knew he would want to be in on this. I set out on snowshoes for the half-mile trek, welcoming the chance to try to absorb the events of the night. In the starlight the trail was only faintly visible. The cold that tore at my lungs was making the trees pop, the only sound that broke the silence. A meteor shot toward the horizon, where the dark form of Tom's cabin loomed.

Tom was a bit startled by my greeting: "Hurry! There's a wolf in our house!" and was ready to go before I had a chance to tell him the whole story.

Meanwhile, Gary was getting things ready in case the wolf got more active. He put more wood in the stove, partitioned off the living room as best he could, and put breakable things aside. By the time Tom and I arrived, the thin chunks of ice that had covered the wolf's fur had melted off. We watched him sit up, look around, and walk over to the small space between the lounge and the stove. He lay down there, his head and shoulders leaning against the lounge, facing us.

The three of us sat in the kitchen, whispering, wanting to bother him as little as possible. We felt excited, awestruck, and I, at least, a bit apprehensive. What was the best thing to do? It was 3:30 on a Saturday morning. We decided to wait until daylight.

Our peeks into the living room were returned by a steady gaze from those bright golden eyes. Pretty soon the presence of a wolf in the living room was irresistible, and we went in to sit on the window bench just to be closer to him.

Quietly, we kept company with the animal that had always seemed to us to represent the essence of wilderness. And we puzzled over the events that might have brought this creature to our home. His radio collar suggested an answer. Maybe he had a history of contact with people that went beyond a single encounter with a wildlife research biologist.

He certainly gave no indication of being upset by our presence. Twice Gary stood beside him to put more wood in the stove, and the wolf continued to lean against the lounge. We know wolves are social animals, able to communicate with facial expressions and posture and vocalizations. But this wolf merely looked about and took a few interested sniffs at pans of water and meat scraps. Still, he was alert to strange human noises: the clattering of pans, the fire burning, our talking. We began to feel hopeful. We had wonderful fantasies about a shy but friendly wolf recuperating with us until ready to return to the wild. We spent long moments just admiring him: the impressive breadth of his handsome head, the lush bunches of face ruff framing those compelling eyes, the grizzled fur luxuriously thick, right down to the black tip of his tail. Until now, our main contact with wolves had been restricted to seeing their tracks along our trails or following the frozen river, so we were especially interested in seeing wolf feet close up. Between long, supple-looking toes grew feathery tufts of reddish fur. And now we could see that he had lost part of a front foot. Had he been unable to hunt because of this? Maybe this was his problem.

But we gradually became aware that his breathing, a little wheezy from the first, was becoming worse. After an hour or so, it was a terrible, deep gurgling.

Gary went over to the lounge and sat on it. Gradually he moved closer until his hand was right beside the wolf's head. Then he stroked his head and ears. There was no reaction that we could see. Gary put a finger under the collar and thought it too tight for an animal having a hard time breathing. So when the wolf finally stood, with some effort, and slumped down to lie flat beside the stove, Gary used the pliers to take off the collar. Throughout this and all the other strange things that happened to him, that wolf never growled or so much as curled a lip at us, as he had so often done to the ravens. Nor did he act afraid.

His well-worn radio collar was inscribed with the number 6530 and an address of the U.S. Fish and Wildlife Service. Thanks to the collar, we were to find that this animal truly was a wild wolf. But more than that, we were to have a fascinating glimpse of his roots.

For more than twenty years research biologist L. David Mech has been studying timber wolves, first in Lake Superior's Isle Royale National Park, and more recently in northern Minnesota. One technique that he and his associates have perfected for wolf studies is radio telemetry. Wolves are trapped, anesthetized, radio-collared, and released. They can be located and observed by people with monitoring equipment. This yields invaluable insights into all aspects of wolf ecology, information that would be difficult or impossible to gain in any other way.

Look back in Mech's records, to December 1973. A female wolf moves through the forest east of northern Minnesota's Iron Range. She has traveled alone for more than a year, roaming across vast stretches of the forested, rocky lake country of Superior National Forest. Her route has encompassed some 2,500 square miles.

An encounter with a wildlife biologist's trap has left her with a radio collar that reveals her locations to aerial researchers and with a number for their records: 2473.

Now she meets a lone male wolf, and together they set up a territory. It meets their needs. Undefended by other wolf packs, its forty square miles provide adequate food for them and their pups. And in this sparsely settled area, activities of people and wolves will seldom conflict. In the spring, she bears their first litter of pups, and they become known to researchers as the Perch Lake Pack.

Four years later the Perch Lake Pack is thriving. Wolf 2473 has a daughter who has become the pack's new alpha, or dominant, female. Her mate is the male who moved in after her father disappeared during the hunting and trapping season of 1974. From now until 1985, these two will be leaders of the pack. They will also be the parents of all the pack's offspring, many of whom will be studied by researchers.

Three pups born in the spring of 1982 were radio-collared. As most young wolves do, they eventually left their home territory, at different times and along varying routes. Male Wolf 6441 left the territory in May 1983, when just over a year old. Eight months later he was killed by a trapper in Ontario, 115 miles to the northeast. Female Wolf 6443 left when she was a year and a half old and settled just southeast of her home territory. She found a mate, but after their effort to raise pups apparently failed, she returned to her home territory alone. Since then she has been in the territory just to the south and west, usually alone.

Their brother, Wolf 6530, stayed with the pack until he was nearly two years old, and then he went traveling. For three months he investigated the forest just to the west. Then he headed northeast, and by August he was near Alice Lake, about forty miles from home. He stayed in this area for five months. Researchers hoped that he would find a mate here and establish his own territory. But early in 1985 he returned to the Perch Lake Pack; he remained with them for two months, passing the date of his third birthday. By June he was back at his Alice Lake hunting grounds.

That same month, on a canoe trip in the Boundary Waters Canoe Area, we were thrilled to find fresh wolf tracks and droppings on a portage that we later learned was just three miles from a point mapped by researchers for Wolf 6530 at that time. Much as we would like to think that our paths crossed then, we had seen wolf signs in that area in previous seasons. It is possible that while there Wolf 6530 found himself unwelcome in territory already occupied by a pack, and that that is why he resumed his travels. Aerial tracking spotted him twenty miles to the southwest in July, fifteen miles farther in August, and twelve more miles to the southwest and very close to his home territory by September.

But later that month, Wolf 6530 covered the distance back to the Alice Lake area, and he was still there in October. Then his signal was lost. His whereabouts were unknown until he found the frozen deer carcasses at our place, twenty-five miles southeast of his last recorded location and forty-five miles east of the Perch Lake Pack.

Now young, well-traveled Wolf 6530 lay on our floor, frightfully sick. His breath came in growling wheezes. Again he got up, painfully, and leaned right against the stove. The smell of singed hair filled the room as Gary rushed to pull him away. The wolf staggered to the center of the room and collapsed.

Three times he stretched across the floor in rigid spasm. After each horrible rattling breath came a terrifying moment of no breath. Then, convulsively, a gurgling gasp. But he hadn't the strength to cough and clear his lungs. He wasn't getting enough oxygen. His lips and tongue turned blue. We sat close beside him and strained with him as he struggled to breathe.

He pawed at his mouth. He tried to get up, and did, partway. He lay with his head up and breathed more easily, but then came another convulsive wave. We hung on each long moment between the breathing out and gasping in. But then one of the moments stretched out way too long, and Gary's touch could no longer stir him. Kneeling by his head we could see his eyes change. The focus was lost, and the yellow faded as the pupils became huge. We could look way into them and see the sunrise light reflected in a green blaze.

We sat there a long time, grieving. And we looked at him closely. A thick winter coat had hidden the extent of his emaciation. Beneath it his bones protruded. He weighed fifty-five pounds but should have weighed at least seventy-five. There was a tear on his lower lip, an old wound. His feet were supple, the pads squeezable and spongy beneath their calloused surfaces, and the fur tufts between his toes were silky. The wolf's right foot had lost three pads. On the left foot one pad was mutilated. These, too, were old wounds, noted in Mech's records since 1983. Mech believes they were probably the result of the wolf's getting caught in a fox trap, pulling the trap loose, and wearing it until the toes sloughed off, a hazard for all Minnesota wolves during the trapping season.

We went out to see what the wolf's tracks could tell us about his last night. We found that although he had wandered all over the woods behind the clearing during the previous week and had made seven beds there, this last night was the only time that he had come toward the house. He had walked to the base of the toboggan run and had climbed all the way up the long, steep hill and then followed the snowshoe trail around behind the building.

There he stood, then turned and went back down to the clearing. Later, he had curled up under the big spruce tree just long enough to make a slight depression in the snow. Then he came up the hill again, all the way up that steep killer of a hill, taking small steps but no sitting stops until he was again behind the house. There he shook himself, and bits of lichen and twigs that had clung to

his fur flew across the snow. Then he turned onto the terrace, walking close beside the house, and squeezed between the bench and the house, where a tuft of woolly wolf hair still hangs from a bent nail. And then he was at the window with that haunting wolf face and those insistent thumps.

After our outing we were more puzzled than ever about what might have prompted the wolf's visit. He had spent so much energy when there must have been little energy left. If it was a random, delirious act, it seemed more likely for him to have gone in any direction but up that steep hill. We snowshoed out to the road and drove to town to call Dave Mech, hoping for some answers.

Mech knew exactly who we were talking about. The wanderings of Wolf 6530 had been of great interest to him, and this information about the wolf's final travels and death would be a valuable addition to his records. An autopsy later revealed that this wolf had died of a fungal pneumonia, and Mech was able to document a natural cause of death that had been virtually unknown among wild wolves. To have contracted the pneumonia, Wolf 6530 must have been stressed in some way. Quite possibly he was undernourished to begin with. Prey animals—few and far between here—are hard to come by in the winter, especially for a lone wolf suffering the nagging pain of an old injury.

We were intrigued by the story of the Perch Lake Pack. And it was a comfort to know more about Wolf 6530. We had developed a deep feeling for him from just one short but intense experience. His story gave us more of him to know.

Mech was able to say something about the great mystery of why the wolf came to the house. Incredible as it seems, he said, it is not at all unknown for starving wild animals to come to human habitation: wolves, raccoons, bobcats, and bears have all approached people near the end. Perhaps these animals sensed warmth or food. Yet these explanations don't adequately fit this case. The house is too far from the clearing for warmth to be felt. As for food, there was still plenty of meat left on the deer carcass in the clearing, and prospects for more.

We'll never know what motivated him to come our way. I can only say that I'm grateful to Wolf 6530 for sharing his last, desperate moments of life. His act gave us a sense of connection with his world that we would never have had, and our commitment to live in harmony with that world has been strengthened. We will always carry with us the vivid image of the wolf at the window.

DEER TICK

actual size

WHITE-FOOTED
MOUSE

engorged

SOMETHING SCARY LURKS OUT THERE

TEXT BY EDWARD R. RICCIUTI • DRAWING BY GLENN WOLFF

It's a gorgeous summer day in northern Westchester County, where New York suburbanites reside among forested hills and fields. It's a grand day for a gambol in the great outdoors. But Westchesterites, as well as residents of suburbs and semirural areas in several other parts of the country, are increasingly jittery nowadays about the outdoors. Thickets and woodlands have become places to be avoided. Something scary lurks out there, even in the bushes at the edge of the lawn.

The specter they fear is a creature not much bigger than the period at the end of this sentence. The main culprit in most of the country is the deer tick, *Ixodes dammini.* With its bite it spreads a disease that some researchers luridly say would be the plague of the 1980s, were it not for AIDS. A close relative, *I. pacificus,* is the key vector on the West Coast. A few other types of ticks also appear to be implicated, but to a much lesser degree.

Lyme disease, named after the southeastern Connecticut town where it was first identified in 1975, has become the most prevalent tick-borne illness in the country—and is spreading. The more time people spend outdoors in areas where Lyme disease is prevalent, the higher the risk they will contract it.

The majority of cases so far have occurred in the Northeast, especially in Connecticut, New York, Rhode Island, Massachusetts, and New Jersey. Wisconsin and Minnesota constitute another critical area, and cases are increasing along the Middle Atlantic seaboard and on the West Coast. The disease has been reported from a total of forty-three states, more than double the number in 1980. Overseas, Lyme disease has cropped up on every continent but Antarctica.

Lyme disease is not considered particularly life-threatening—although a few deaths from complications may have occurred—but it can produce painful, debilitating symptoms that make for a lifetime of misery. If diagnosed early, Lyme disease is readily treatable with antibiotics such as penicillin or tetracycline. The problem is that sometimes it goes undetected.

Lyme disease is caused by *Borrelia burgdorferi,* a whip-tailed bacterium that infects the blood and tissues of dozens of mammals which are hosts for ticks. Songbirds and groundbirds can carry the germ too. Dogs, unlike these wild animal hosts, can develop Lyme disease symptoms when they become carriers.

Deer ticks have a two-year life cycle. Larvae hatch in late spring and summer and attach themselves to small mammals and birds, but seldom people. Larvae molt into nymphs the next spring and find hosts, especially the white-footed mouse and other small rodents—and, very often, humans. The nymphs stay close to the ground. At summer's end, the nymphs become adults, which climb into the brush and attach themselves to deer and people. The proliferation of white-tailed deer has been linked to the spread of the disease. So have environmental restrictions on pesticides and the burning of brush, although the evidence is inconclusive.

Ticks ingest bacteria along with a blood meal from infected animals. The bacteria head for the tick gut, from which they can be transmitted to a human host. It seems to take several hours for a tick to transmit the disease, so removal of ticks upon discovery is a first-line preventative.

Human infection is usually signaled by the appearance of a rash within a month of the bite. Circular, and clear in the center, it resembles a red bull's-eye. It can spread until it covers an area that is larger than a dinner plate. Even after the rash appears, the disease is easily zapped by antibiotics. Unfortunately, the rash does not show up in 30 percent of the victims.

Antibiotics usually work against the disease, even in later stages. The problem with diagnosing the disease later on, however, is that by then its symptoms mimic those of many other illnesses; hence, Lyme disease is frequently called the "great imitator." When the first serious outbreak occurred in and

35

around Lyme, Connecticut, it was believed to be arthritis. Early on, the disease was often referred to as Lyme arthritis.

Cases of Lyme disease vary greatly in severity. Some victims feel no more discomfort than if they had a mild case of flu. Many others develop nausea, stiff neck, and inflamed joints with pain similar to that caused by arthritis. That's the worst most people get. But a small percentage can be in for real trouble. The bacteria can attack the heart, causing heart block and other disorders that can make installation of a pacemaker necessary. They can also invade the nervous system, producing symptoms like those of meningitis and encephalitis. Fierce headaches, facial paralysis, and such psychological changes as depression and temporary loss of memory also can occur. Loss of muscular coordination sometimes makes the disease seem like multiple sclerosis.

Especially in regions where Lyme disease is new, and thus not recognized as such, victims sometimes spend years under treatment for the wrong sickness. Public health authorities have mounted major campaigns to familiarize physicians, and the public, with Lyme disease and its signs.

Awareness is one of the reasons that cases reported to state health agencies have increased. About 14,000 cases are officially on record since 1980, 5,000 in 1988 alone. But health officials in key Lyme disease states say that number is only a fraction of the true total.

To go officially on record as Lyme disease, a case must meet several federal standards and criteria. A serologic test must show antibodies to the bacterium. Certain symptoms, such as the rash, must also be present. Because of the variability of the disease, the right symptoms may not show up, and the serologic test doesn't always work—especially after early antibiotic treatment. There are slight indications that some strains of the bacteria may evade the test, and be more virulent to boot. Reporting systems are far from perfect, too, even in states where Lyme disease is concentrated, because the outbreak is a relatively new phenomenon.

A reservoir of Lyme disease has been around for a long time, however, especially abroad. Only recently has it overflowed into newsworthy proportions. European medical literature almost a century ago described the Lyme disease rash—technically called erythema chronicum migrans, or ECM—as "a chronic red rash that spreads." Some old reports associated the rash with other symptoms, but the link was tenuous.

ECM was first linked to tick bite in the United States five years before Lyme disease was identified. A Wisconsin physician developed the rash after he was bitten by a tick while hunting grouse. He then experienced aches and fever so severe he was hospitalized. Fellow physicians could not determine the cause of his problem until the Milwaukee dermatologist Dr. R.J. Scrimenti connected the tick bite with the rash, a feat for which he is seldom credited in Lyme disease literature. He published a report to alert other doctors, but it was largely ignored.

Then came the Connecticut episode that gave the disease its name. Mysteriously, a cluster of thirty-nine children and twelve adults in and around the lower Connecticut River Valley town of Lyme developed what appeared to be rheumatoid arthritis. Juvenile rheumatoid arthritis is extremely rare, and the incidence in Lyme was one hundred times the normal rate. Medical researchers from Yale University began an investigation that eventually tied together the arthritis-like symptoms, ECM, and tick bite. Picking up the chain of vectors at the ticks, Dr. Willy Burgdorfer, at the Rocky Mountain Laboratories in Hamilton, Montana, isolated the Lyme disease bacterium in 1981.

Many observers have noted curious circumstantial parallels between Lyme disease and AIDS. Both seem to have existed for some time but suddenly and mysteriously exploded into frightening prominence. Like AIDS, Lyme disease may be transmittable directly by infected blood. A Wisconsin hunter came down with it after he cut himself while dressing a deer. Many people test positive for Lyme disease but have no symptoms—another eerie resonance of AIDS—but, in theory, become a vector themselves.

There has been some concern that mosquitoes could spread both Lyme disease and AIDS, although researchers play down the possibility. At the Connecticut Agricultural Research Station in New Haven, a center of study on Lyme disease ecology, the Lyme bacterium has been found in tissues of horseflies and mosquitoes. However, Dr. John F. Anderson, the entomologist who is director of the center, says the infectious agent does not grow when the tissue is cultured in a test tube nor do flying insects seem able to infect people with Lyme disease.

Again, as with AIDS, Lyme disease has hit hardest at a particular segment of society. Here the analogy begins to break down and to give way to irony. Victims of AIDS are primarily active male homosexuals and intravenous drug users, particularly among minorities. Lyme disease, on the other hand, has been characterized as a "suburban disease." Most hard-hit areas are suburban, like Westchester County, or are semirural, growing toward suburbia, like Lyme. Deer ticks thrive, and Lyme disease is common, on certain resort islands that are the summer homes of the rich and famous, such as Nantucket, Massachusetts, and Shelter Island, New York.

The impact of Lyme disease on Establishment interests, says one federal researcher, has prompted media attention, perhaps more than is warranted. He is Dr. Ben Schwartz, an epidemiologist at the Centers for Disease Control (CDC) in Atlanta, Georgia. Schwartz stresses that the CDC considers Lyme disease a "major concern," but he cautions against suggestions that it approaches AIDS as a public-health problem. "Everyone dies from AIDS," he says. "People don't die from Lyme disease."

Residential development in wooded areas, say researchers, not only brings more people into contact with ticks but creates optimum habitat for ticks and their mammalian hosts. Deer ticks, and their host mice and whitetails, flourish most when vegetation is in transition and diverse. Wildlife managers intentionally create this so-called "edge effect" by cutting clearings in forest. Developers unwittingly do it by putting lawns in the woods.

Among the other ironies of Lyme disease is the suburban syndrome. City people head for the "country" but often don't like everything they find there, such as chainsaws droning on Sunday mornings or pigs on the farm next-door. Eventually, the country becomes the suburbs.

Suburbanites want the woods, but most want them friendly. Lyme disease ticks are unfriendly, and one reason they are infecting so many people is that people are coming to ticks.

Concentrating people in prime habitat for ticks and their wild hosts can cause the clusters of cases typical of Lyme disease. Children, spouses, and neighbors are afflicted. People panic. By and large, it appears that fear of Lyme disease is more rampant among suburbanites than among the truly country and woodsy types, even in the same area. The good old boys from the rod and gun clubs, hard-core birders, and big-country backpackers are still out there in the bushes. But they check themselves for ticks at day's end. If bitten, they see a physician, who may administer antibiotics immediately. And that's that.

Lyme disease has changed the perception that many people in afflicted areas have of nature. Comfortably situated Americans

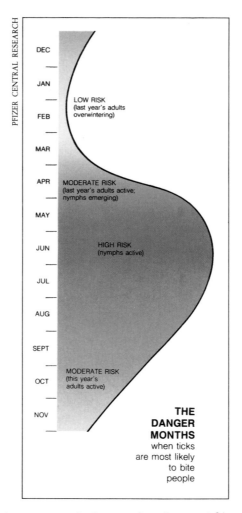

PFIZER CENTRAL RESEARCH

DEC

JAN

FEB

LOW RISK
(last year's adults
overwintering)

MAR

APR

MODERATE RISK
(last year's adults active;
nymphs emerging)

MAY

JUN

HIGH RISK
(nymphs active)

JUL

AUG

SEPT

OCT

MODERATE RISK
(this year's
adults active)

NOV

**THE
DANGER
MONTHS**
when ticks
are most likely
to bite
people

have come to look upon deer the way African peasants view the elephants that trample their corn—as a menace that humans must control, without mercy, in order to survive. That happened in a neighborhood of Ipswich, Massachusetts, a well-heeled community on the North Shore above Boston.

The neighborhood centers on Argilla Road, where many residents have substantial amounts of land around their expensive homes. The road leads to 2,100 dedicated acres fronting on the ocean: the Crane Memorial Reservation and Crane Wildlife Refuge, named for a prominent family living in the area. During the 1970s deer protected in "Crane's Beach" began to multiply.

Neighborhood people enjoyed and protected the deer. The town had some of the most restrictive local hunting regulations in the state. Deer continued to increase. The Massachusetts Division of Fisheries and Wildlife took notice. The agency advised the Trustees of Reservations, a nonprofit organization responsible for nearly 20,000 acres of land in the Bay State, that the Crane's Beach deer population was growing too large for the habitat to support. In 1983 the agency proposed that the Trustees allow a controlled deer hunt on the area during the regular season.

The hunt was resisted by many residents and animal-rights groups. But it was finally initiated in 1985. By then much had changed. Forty percent of the residents in the Argilla Road neighborhood had contracted Lyme disease. Deer, once valued as part of the area's rural character, became objects of fear, lepers of the animal kingdom.

"To coexist with deer has become a nightmare," one Argilla Road resident, Alice W. Shurcliff, wrote to *Audubon* Magazine a few months ago in response to an article on white-tailed deer. Shurcliff, a retired economist, is active in a local group that is pressing the state legislature for home-rule powers to open a year-round deer season for Ipswich landowners. She "used to have sympathy" with animal-rightists, she says. "I used to think that way myself." But Lyme disease has "changed our whole feeling about the outdoors," she explains. Her brother, the physicist William A. Shurcliff (who was an early leader in the historic fight to prevent development of an American supersonic transport plane), contracted Lyme disease and now seldom visits his country house in Ipswich.

Backed by the Ipswich town fathers, Shurcliff's group—the Lyme Disease Study Group—has worked diligently for the year-round deer hunt.

Testifying before a joint committee of the state legislature on behalf of the home-rule petition, Shurcliff asked, "What could be more damaging to one's property . . . than to have all the pleasure of sitting on the front lawn and working in the garden taken away from us? To worry about little children playing on the lawn? We do not want to share our lawns with deer any longer."

The campaign by the Ipswich group has been strongly opposed by the Massachusetts Division of Fisheries and Wildlife. It says that approval of the petition would undermine the division's authority to set hunting seasons without political interference. Again irony. Anti-hunting groups have often attempted to achieve that end by pressing for local control over wildlife regulations. Because of their opposition to the year-round hunt, state wildlife managers find themselves on the same side as anti-hunters.

In the eyes of the Ipswich Lyme disease group, "we've gone from deer killers to deer lovers," says Wayne MacCallum, assistant director in charge of research for the wildlfe division. "Our object is to maintain and perpetuate a healthy deer herd. Unregulated removal of deer won't do that."

The deer problem was addressed by researchers at an international meeting on Lyme disease convened in the fall of 1987 by the New York Academy of Sciences. A Harvard School of Public Health scientist familiar with the Ipswich situation noted that, short of blowing all deer to extinction, elimination of deer from one area is practical only under special circumstances, such as when the herd is surrounded by a deer-proof fence. Otherwise, more deer will simply move in.

Lyme disease experts concede, however, that careful management of deer herds helps. Scientists from the New Jersey State Department of Health noted that major outbreaks occur where deer populations are not adequately managed. Collisions between whitetails and cars have quadrupled, and crop damage is especially high in Garden State municipalities where deer management through hunting is prohibited, the researchers added. They concluded that this trio of problems could make management practices in such areas less controversial.

Other potential control methods include the burning of brush, but that works only in small areas, and the relief it brings is temporary. Pesticides may kill adult ticks on leafless brush in the fall, but they do not penetrate the vegetation to get at the nymphs earlier in the season. Besides, pesticide application has environmental ramifications.

Recently, Harvard researchers developed a device aimed at tick larvae that seems promising, although it has not been widely tested. Cotton treated with a pesticide (an acaricide intended for use on mites) is placed in a biodegradable tube and left for white-footed mice to take as nesting material. Tick larvae that feed on mice may spend up to eight months in their nests after dropping off the host. The treated cotton has long-term killing power against the larvae but seems not to harm the mice.

For now, experts say the best way to protect yourself against Lyme disease is to wear long sleeves, tuck in your trousers, use tick repellent on clothing, and check yourself for ticks. If you have been bitten, contact a physician. No matter where you live, keep an eye out for ticks. Lyme disease isn't going to go away, nor are the ticks.

In 1754, after returning from a three-year study of natural history in America, the Swedish naturalist Pehr Kalm wrote this about the ticks he encountered in the Hudson River Valley: "This small vile creature may, in the future, cause the inhabitants of this land great damage unless a method is discovered which will prevent it from increasing at such a shocking rate."

II
BIRDS OF MANY FEATHERS

THE ANCIENT FAITH

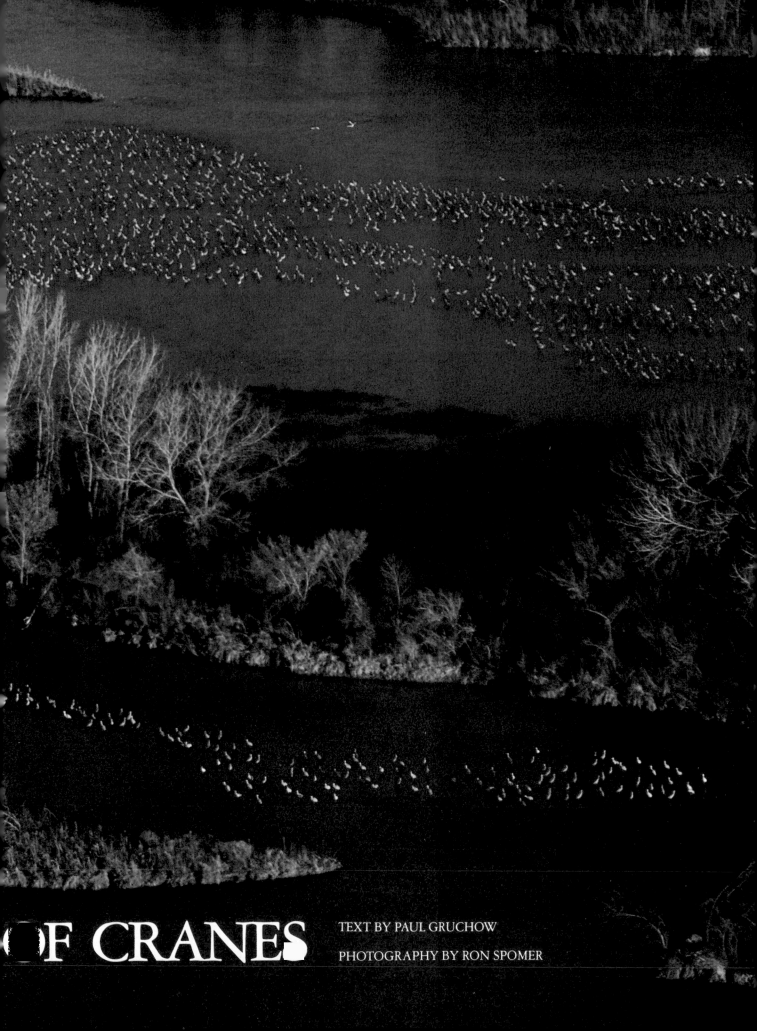

OF CRANES

TEXT BY PAUL GRUCHOW

PHOTOGRAPHY BY RON SPOMER

The travel alarm clock sounded at 4:30 A.M.
and wound down before I could find it on
the unfamiliar nightstand in the cheap motel
room in Grand Island, Nebraska. I fought
consciousness as a drowning man does water.
Then I remembered where I was and why. I
massaged my eyes with my knuckles,
switched on the blinding light, got up,
stumbled toward the bathroom. I dressed
warmly—jeans, thick woolen socks, insulated
boots, heavy shirt, sweater, winter jacket,
stocking cap, gloves—and went out onto the
balcony. Stars glimmered through the haze
of city lights. The day promised to be hot—
temperatures in the high eighties were
predicted—but it was still freezing, and I
knew I would be grateful for my heavy
clothes. I headed my car westward, stopped
for a cup of coffee, put the lights of the prairie town and what little traffic there was behind me. I was in search of sandhill cranes.

At the first slumbering village I took a
country road south, past the bright lights of
an Interstate 80 truck stop. The road arched
over the highway and descended into a region of bottomlands, of meadows, of gravel
mines, of willow and cottonwood thickets, a

closed-in place more reminiscent of Missouri
than of wide-open Nebraska. I crossed a
skinny bridge. The channel of water it
spanned was not the main channel of the
Platte River. Its flow was too narrow, too direct. But in the faint light of the new day, I
could see sandhill cranes downriver, emerging from the water like the pilings of some
abandoned, improbable ruin.

I pulled onto a meadow road at the far
edge of the channel, shut off the engine.
Scarcely had I cracked the window when the
primeval sound rushed in, halfway between a
croak and a song, the music of dry bones rattling. It surged and fell in a regular rhythm,
like waves washing against a shore. I had last
heard the cranes a year before in another
place, but it seemed as if their rattles had
never completely dissipated. The sound of
the sandhill cranes is like the roaring of the
sea in a conch shell; when you finally hear it,
you recognize that you have always known it.
It is like the cry of a loon or the howling of
wolves or the warning rattle of a snake, an article in the universal language.

The blades of last year's grass were stiff
with frost. They cracked underfoot like plas-

tic trinkets. It was almost too early for bird-song. The river gurgled and sucked. The cranes, standing halfway to their knees in the frigid water, cried and cried. As it happened, it was Good Friday. My ears heard cranes, and my heart heard lamentations.

The main channel of the Platte was still nearly a mile away, but I could hear the cranes there too, in far greater numbers. At the rim of the horizon, the sky began to lighten. The sound of the birds was hauling up the curtain of day. Blackbirds trilled in the willows. A crow cackled. A pair of wood ducks flew low over the water, their wings squeaking against the air underneath. In the hayfield, a meadowlark sang a song as crisp as a bugle call. Matins on Good Friday morning. At the edge of the river, in an eddy around the roots of a cottonwood tree, the carcass of a raccoon rocked gently back and forth in a cradle of death. It was beginning to be light enough to see the yellow blush of life in the supple trunks of the willows.

The cranes stood like a congregation in the shallows of the river. I could see their long necks now, could watch them stalk about as if on tiptoe, could observe them stretching and

settling their wings. Already some of their brethren from the sandbars farther south had taken flight, heading from the river to the fields nearby to feed for the day. They showed the characteristic profile of the cranes, necks straight out, legs tucked in, feet trailing behind like rudders. The morning was approaching when they would have fed long enough along the Platte, when they would rise into the air and not descend again until they had reached their nesting grounds on the tundra.

Behind me, car doors slammed. I turned from my crouch in the shadow of a cotton-wood tree. Three persons, a man, a woman, and a boy, stood at the edge of the road, binoculars dangling from their necks, their bare hands tucked into jeans pockets. This arrival stirred the nervous birds, and the volume of their calling intensified. Half a dozen of them stretched their wings, took to the air, and circled the flock in the river below, beckoning the rest. But most of the cranes stuck to the roost.

We were gathered at a great transcontinental crossroads. The wide, many-channeled river, running from west to east, from the

43

mountains to the Missouri, defined one axis, the highway of the sun. The cranes, traveling from south to north and back again, from the Gulf to the Arctic, defined the other, the highway of the winds. Here at the center of the continent the two great streams of traffic met and mixed.

The way west cut across the grain of the continent, across its mountains, across the Mississippi running down its midsection. It had long been the way of humans. The Pawnees followed the river before the Europeans came, and when the new settlers headed west, their roads also followed it, as ours do now. The four of us were standing on Mormon Island, named for the trail just to the north of us that the disciples of Brigham Young took to Utah. Just to the south ran the old Oregon Trail, the river of the westward movement, of the gold rush, of Manifest Destiny. Later the Pony Express route ran that way, then the railroads and the telegraph wires. The roar of traffic along a modern interstate highway a mile away carried even above the wild sound of cranes. These vehicles were part of a stream of traffic that began centuries ago and has run unabated, although increasingly swiftly, ever since. Overhead, the contrail of a jet arced westward.

The continent itself stretched along the north–south axis, the way of the winds and of the great animal migrations, the way of songbirds, of waterbirds, of monarch butterflies, of bison, of polar bears, of whales, of sandhill cranes, of creatures great and small moving in concert with the seasons, which also followed the northward and southward tiltings of the Earth on its axis.

For every century that humans have traversed the mile-wide Platte, there has been a millennium of crane flight. In the few centuries of our intersection we have, it seems, been moving not only in counter-directions but also at cross-purposes. The differences lie neither in the nature of cranes nor in that of humans, but in our different ways of occupying and using land. The flyways of the cranes are the paths of nomads. Our highways are the routes of settlement or, more precisely, of occupation.

The nomad is a visitor but not a stranger, one whose visit is a kind of embrace. I do not mean that it is innocent or without consequences but only that it is temporary. It is a way of taking hold of the land, even of exploiting it, without altering its essential character. The nomad lives necessarily within the limits of the land and cannot take more from it than the land itself offers at the moment of the visit. The nomad receives the fruits of the land as a gift to its journey.

Occupation, on the other hand, is a form of exclusion, and it is possible to practice exclusion without limits. The occupier receives the land not as a gift but as a commodity, as a right rather than a privilege. To the extent that the occupier recognizes limits, they are primarily practical. Morality has proved, with respect to the land at least, a less powerful restraint than necessity.

When we gave up our nomadic ways, we gained a certain freedom from the limits of the land, although it may yet prove to have been illusory. In his youthful vision, the Dakota prophet Black Elk correctly saw a river of occupation running from east to west, and he saw that it was the color of spilled blood. The blood, of course, was that of his own people, but it was also the blood of the bison, upon which his people depended utterly. He saw instinctively, as we do not, that the death of the land and the death of the culture were inextricably linked.

The four of us stood our respectful distances and watched the ancient race of cranes at their morning rituals, at their nervous dancing, their strutting, their preening and repairing of feathers, their raucous chattering. The sun rose. It popped up abruptly as it always does along distant horizons, on the prairies or at sea. Suddenly the long reach of the sun fell upon us, warm as a heat lamp, and cast shadows far behind us. The crystals of frost on the blades of meadow grass sparkled. Everything was bathed in the warm backlight. The fields were golden, the waters like willow-plate china, the willows as brilliant as the appendages of the yellowlegs.

The other onlookers shivered and retreated. Doors banged. The car's engine turned and caught. The machine sped away in a spray of gravel. They had taken no notice of me, and I had paid scant attention to them, but I was glad they were gone.

Half of the cranes took to the air noisily, circled above the river, and headed north into the pastures and cornfields on the far side of the highway. I lingered briefly, but with the sun the spell of the birds had melted. Alone, I resented the earlier company all the more. I felt as if I had been interrupted at prayer.

I got into my own car and returned to the city. Its inhabitants rushed toward places of commerce, running yellow warning lights, honking, yielding their hard-earned places in the pack to no one. I could no more comprehend the impatient daily migration of my own kind than I could the ageless flight of the cranes.

I headed west in the heat of day toward North Platte, 180 miles upriver. The road

followed the river flats through a succession of farming towns along the edge of the Nebraska sandhills. The sandhills stretch a hundred miles to the north, an almost unknown region of dunes and grazed grasses and of the yucca plant called soapweed. They are one of the empty places in the North American landscape, the largest unstabilized complex of sand dunes on the continent.

The dunes were formed during the last major period of glaciation, the Wisconsin, which ended in Nebraska about twenty thousand years ago. Strong westerly winds carried the fine, glacier-ground loess soils eastward, creating the foundation for what is now the fertile Corn Belt and leaving behind the heavier deposits of sand and gravel. The sands make, in western and central Nebraska, a sensuous landscape, tan and rounded like a succession of bellies, supine. Driving it is like riding across a chart of brain waves. In the hills the road signs mark ranches, not towns. To the south, across the

thousand feet wide, sandbars free of vegetation, and roosts where the water is no more than six inches deep. Once, too, the river was bounded by extensive meadows rich in crane forage: in snails and snakes, frogs and worms, the tubers of marsh plants. A crane needs to gain a pound of weight on the Platte to make the next leg of its journey to the Arctic for the summer nesting season.

These days 70 percent of the water that once poured down the Platte in springtime is diverted before it ever reaches Nebraska. Some of it goes into reservoirs, some into irrigation canals; some is claimed to manufacture electrical power. Only west of North Platte and again west of Grand Island, where a portion of the diverted water reenters the river, does the Platte retain a semblance of its historical character and offer resting and feeding places suitable for cranes.

The heat descended as promised. I remembered driving across these same plains farther south in Kansas in an August when the whole land from South Dakota to the Gulf was caught in the grip of a suffocating drought. Sparks from the wheels of passing trains set off grass fires. Some of the golden wheat still stood. Other fields had already been reaped, and the windrows of yellow straw blazed like the ruins of a battlefield. Smoke and the sweet smell of ashes blanketed everything.

I remembered happening upon a settlement on a knoll. It was scarcely even a village. A few houses, an elevator, a gas station. Mostly it was given over to an enormous cemetery. The striking thing about the cemetery was not that there were so many graves, but that the spaces between them were so wide. These people needed as much elbowroom in death as in life. The grass in the wide avenues between the gravestones had been cut and cured and stacked. The stacks looked like loaves of bread. I could not tell whether I was seeing a cemetery that had been harvested or a hayfield with burial markers. And the accumulation of graves did seem incredible. How could so many have died in a place where so few had lived?

Back in Nebraska the rays of the sun streamed through the windshield and concentrated in the car. Inside it was like August. The heat reminded me of that cemetery in Kansas, and so did the little towns I passed through—weedy, unpainted, boarded up, more like cemetery towns than living organisms. I rolled up the windows, turned on the air conditioner, and sped on toward North Platte, bored with the road and eager to be settled in for the night. It was already dark by the time I had checked in, un-

river, rises a line of taller, blue hills, and beyond them lie the wide, flat plains, inclining imperceptibly toward the Rocky Mountains.

For the first sixty miles, until I reached Lexington, the sky was dotted with cranes riding the spring thermals. The fields were speckled with them. After Lexington, the cranes disappeared. Once, all of the Platte River, which runs 330 miles across Nebraska, was familiar ground to the sandhill cranes and their nearly extinct cousins, the whooping cranes. But the cranes now stop along only the eighty-mile stretch between Grand Island and Lexington, and the twenty miles from North Platte west to Sutherland.

For centuries each springtime, the meltwaters of Wyoming surged down the Platte, scouring it of trees and brush and creating wide, clear channels of water and fresh islands of sand on which the birds could roost at night, safe from the preying of coyotes, foxes, and, in more recent times, dogs. To feel safe, cranes need channels at least two packed, and napped, too late for watching cranes, but I got into my car and headed west again anyway. I needed to be reassured that I could find them where I always had.

I passed the bright lights of the biggest rail-switching yard in the nation; here trains from the East divide before they tackle the Rockies. At the sign advertising the potter's studio, I turned right toward the river, which I could sense but not see. I missed the next turn and found myself stopped in the narrow lane by several cows that had escaped through their fence. They were transfixed by my headlights. I flicked the lights, cranked down the window, shouted at them, honked the horn. They were uncontrollably curious, as cows always are, and completely unintimidated, the opposite of the nervous cranes. They stared at me, moon-faced, and would not budge. I was resigned to getting out and forcibly shooing them away when they finally relented, casting sideways glances at me out of their doleful eyes, and ambled slowly into the ditch, permitting me to pass.

At the farmyard just up the way, I pulled in and circled back. A German shepherd with a savage bark bounded out of the darkness and gave fierce chase. I was glad to be encased in metal. The night was taking a sinister turn. I had come searching for the reassurance of something ancient and gotten myself entangled instead in the complicated mesh of civilization.

I found the right intersection, and the next one, saw the familiar house standing too high on its foundation, passed it to the place where the road curves along the canal, shut off the engine, turned out the lights, and opened the window. The prehistoric rattle of sandhill cranes at roost filled the night air. I could not see them. I didn't need to. I knew exactly where they were, and where they would be tomorrow, and where they would be next year at the same hour. I search out the cranes every spring for precisely this reason: because they can be counted upon, because their lives are predictable, their movements regular, their habits ordered. It is as comforting to know that the cranes have come back to the Platte in March as to feel the blood pulsing through the veins in my own wrists. It is a tangible sign that all is still well with the world.

One of the habits of naturalists is the recording of phenology. A science can be made of the meticulous mapping of patterns of climate against coinciding cycles of biological phenomena. I know by consulting my own charts that the leopard frogs migrated from Mudhole Bay on Lake Okabena in Worthington, Minnesota, on the night of

April 6, 1986, about two weeks later than the muskrats emerged from their winter dens and about two weeks earlier than the thirteen-lined ground squirrels first appeared. Seven frogs were killed that night by passing automobiles.

Were I to keep similar records over decades, I might be able to say something definitive about the life and population cycles of leopard frogs in Worthington as they relate to climate; and it is possible that this information could contribute in some unforeseen way to a clearer understanding of life in general. Charles Darwin, after all, spent twenty years studying the life histories of English barnacles before he was ready to write his theory of the natural selection of species, and Alfred Kinsey needed what he had learned from an exhaustive study of the taxonomy of North American grasshoppers to undertake his revolutionary examination of the sexual practices of North American humans.

But I do not keep such records in the cause of science. Nor do I drive the length of Nebraska every springtime and go to exactly the same place along the Platte River to watch the sandhill cranes because I am under the delusion that in doing so I will learn something undiscovered about them. If I were after information not already known to me, I would stay home, visit the library, request a computer printout of the references in the technical literature. I would try for a grant, proposing to study the role of the lesser sandhill crane in the life-cycle of some parasite of the pond snail, *Stagnicola elodes.* I would learn to operate a radio homing device and prepare to follow the sandhill cranes north to their nesting grounds. I would do something, anything, systematic. There is nothing systematic about driving to North Platte, Nebraska, even repeatedly, and rolling down the car window.

You may record the phenology of frogs and sunflowers and cranes, but it is not possible, as naturalist Ann Zwinger has said, to track that of your children. Their lives are not cyclical, as lives in nature appear to be. Your children do not come back in the same form to the same place season after season. The best you can expect from children, the thing you hope for, pray for, is that they will grow and change, that each year will be for them new and different, an advancement. We live out our lives along a linear progression we cannot forecast.

But I am confident that there will be sandhill cranes along the Platte River during the second week of March in 1999, and I would confidently predict that there will be sandhill cranes along the same river in the same month of 2099, as there have been these past millions of years, were it not for human beings and their unpredictable interventions.

As for myself, I cannot say with any degree of certainty where I will be in March of 1991, or what I will be doing, or why. My own life does not seem to me inevitable. It is not orderly. It has never been logical. But we want logic and order in our lives. We long to see the structure in things. We search for patterns. We look for constancies.

I have been visiting a friend who has Alzheimer's disease. One morning she came into her living room, looked at a brass teapot sitting on the mantel of her fireplace, where a beam of morning sunlight was striking it, and said, "Oh! Isn't that a beautiful teapot!"—as though she had never seen it before.

"Yes," I said. "Where did you get it?"

"Get what?"

"The teapot."

She looked puzzled. "What is a teapot?" she asked.

I pointed it out to her, but it was no use. She had already forgotten the connection between the word "teapot" and the object shining so brightly on the fireplace mantel. Still, it is possible to have transitory conversations with her. The present may be a constant bafflement, but sometimes she can be drawn into memory.

We ourselves seldom comprehend the moment at hand. So we turn to history, the one element of our lives on which it is possible to fix. Or we turn to principle. Or we turn to nature. There we find, amid the silence and mystery, order and structure, the sense that life is not simply random. The sun always rises in the east and sets in the west. Pasqueflowers bloom in April and prairie gentians in September and never the reverse. The spiral of the shell of the right-handed pond snail is always logarithmic. In March the sandhill cranes always return to a certain meadow northwest of North Platte, Nebraska. These are truths we can depend upon.

The next morning, Holy Saturday morning, I returned to the meadow. It was all familiar to me: the narrow canal and its dry bed of sand, thick with the footprints of creatures that had traveled it in the night; the thicket of dried sunflowers along the banks of the canal; the red-winged blackbird warbling on the fencepost; the line of cottonwoods at the edge of the river in the distance; the woodpile in which I had hidden in years past; the sweet song of the meadowlark; the morning air; the long meadow, trim as a golf course, striated with thin puddles of water in which the feathers of cranes floated; the congregations of cranes gathered like drifts of gray snow at the center of the meadow, their voices rising not in one continuous clatter but in waves, like the cheers of a crowd.

I brought a spotting scope. The cranes are loners, nervous and shy. In the Arctic they have been seen to chase full-grown caribou from their nesting grounds. In Nebraska they will flee a human invader while he is still thousands of yards away. They are constantly vigilant. When you can scarcely see them, they have already been long aware of you. Many birds are accustomed to cars and will allow you to drive quite close, but cranes in a cornfield will sometimes flee even at the approach of an automobile. They take no chances. In the air a sandhill crane is somewhat more secure. One will occasionally fly so low over your head that you think you might reach up and touch it. But the only way to get close to a roosting crane is to resort to mechanical contrivances, to a blind or a long lens.

In the reach of the glass, I pulled the cranes toward me, singled out one standing at the edge of the crowd, focused on it. I felt like a person shrouded in a veil, permitted to approach but not on equal terms. From a distance a sandhill crane is a mass of gray, impressive for its size—six or seven pounds, three-and-a-half feet high, wingspan as wide as an average adult male is tall—but rather colorless and awkward, like a pewter pitcher on stilts. In the tiny, round field of the telescopic lens, the bird revealed its fierce ornaments: a mouse-colored wash along the bone line and on the feather tips of its wings; a scarlet cap running from its hooked beak around its eye and across its forehead (the older the bird, the redder the cap); and an eye the color of a raw wound with a piercing black iris.

In the glass too you can see the crane's angular features, its sinewy neck, its scaly legs. The sandhill is an archaic bird—the fossil evidence for it dates back fifty-five million years—and it looks as alien, as sinister and otherworldly, as that last vestige of the dinosaur age, the crocodile. In fact, the brain of a sandhill crane more closely resembles a crocodile's than any mammal's. The architecture of the crane's brain is one of the reasons for believing, as scientists do, that cranes, indeed all birds, have descended from reptiles.

The evidence of the link between birds and reptiles is the fossil *Archaeopteryx,* first discovered in 1861 in a limestone quarry in Bavaria, one of five known specimens. *Archaeopteryx* lived 160 million years ago and was a flying reptile, a crow-sized creature with feathers exactly like those of modern birds and with the wishbone of birds, but with the skeletal features of a reptile: the skull of a dinosaur, a jaw with reptilian teeth, a long bony tail, abdominal and cervical ribs, clawed fingers. (Even now on rare occasions a vestigial claw will appear on the wings of some birds, among them cranes.) "Birds are intense, fast-living creatures—reptiles, I suppose one might say, that have escaped out of the heavy sleep of time, transformed fairy creatures dancing over sunlit meadows," Loren Eiseley said.

The morning had come while I was unawares. I stood, stretched my legs, shook the kinks out of my back. The thousands of cranes in the meadow shrieked in alarm and rose into the air as one body, the force of their wings sounding against the weight of the air like the rolling of a thousand snare drums. They fanned out until they filled the sky and churned forward, their wings wheezing, parting in a circle around me. I stood agape, like the women at the empty tomb. When no sound remained but the champagne music of the redwings, I went to breakfast.

Thinking about it over biscuits and gravy, I realized how wrong I had been. I did in fact know where I would be next March. I would be along the Platte River with the cranes, compelled to return by my own nature as much as they would be by theirs. Perhaps I would be dead by then, of course, but so might they. The odds were that I would be coming to see cranes at this place long after every one of these particular representatives of the species had perished. On average, a human lives fifty years longer than a crane.

I find structure in the life of cranes but not in my own life or in the lives of my children, I realized, because I see cranes in communities but I think of humans individually. The paradox of Easter is the paradox of rebirth. Yet the death and rebirth of a community is not paradoxical. An individual sandhill crane is born, matures, and dies; but the community of cranes returns century after century to the same meadow at the foot of the sandhills along the North Platte River in southern Nebraska. It is this truth, the transcendence of the species over the individual, the way in which a community endures and accumulates a history despite the frailties of the creatures who inhabit it, that we celebrate when we stand in awe before the great seasonal migrations. The story of Easter is not paradoxical either, if we will think of it in the same way; if we will think not of the individual existence, which is fleeting, but of the continuities in the human community—the continuity, despite everything, of human life, of culture, above all, of faith.

Easter morning arose like a dream. I emerged from my room in the hour before dawn, my eyes raw around the edges, taut with the unfulfilled desire for sleep, and found myself bathed in an untimely darkness. The moon had already fallen, and the stars were nowhere to be seen. They were hidden behind great banks of cloud scarcely higher than the tops of the trees, showing a satiny sheen in the gauzy lights of Grand Island. I had driven only a mile or two beyond the city when huge crystals of wet snow began to flutter against the windshield like pieces of confetti, driven on a gentle northwest wind.

By the time I reached the river plain, the snow was falling, or rather raining, in a continuous sheet, and everything was shrouded in it: the dried inflorescences of the sunflowers, the soft layer of sand in the bottom of the canal, the tops of the fenceposts, the limbs of the cottonwoods. It was damp but not bitterly cold. The soft snow feathered the gray landscape. It looked pristine and smelled freshly washed. I felt veiled once again.

Although dawn was near when I took my customary place along the bank of the canal, I could not distinguish the gray cranes from the gray shadows. Their voices rose, muffled by the breeze, and fluttered down like the flakes of snow. For a long time I sat immersed in the sound. It seemed to be everywhere and at the same time a long way off. Minute degree by minute degree the light gathered. The sun rose, invisible behind the thick curtain of clouds. Gradually the faint outlines of cranes emerged from the fleecy shadows through the mists of snow. The birds were restless. Small groups of them took briefly to the air, settled again. The snow collected on my collar, on the backs of my hands, gathered in my eyebrows. It felt wet and cold, like the muzzle of a dog. The longer I sat watching the cranes while the snow drifted over me, the more mysterious their presence seemed.

Why this congregational movement? I understood the principle of safety in numbers, how the cranes as a species were secured from the ravages of predation by moving this way *en masse*. And I understood the influence of place, how the Platte River, so ideally suited to the needs of cranes in migration, should come to serve as a common staging ground. But two subspecies of sandhill cranes, the Mississippi and the Florida, do not migrate at all. How does it benefit their cousins to make such a long journey, and so collectively? How

did it start? What encouraged it to continue? Why did they not, like their cousins, settle down in a single place where they could both live and reproduce? What, exactly, is the long-term gain to the sandhill cranes in this incredible expenditure of energy every spring and fall? What justifies the risks involved in making the trip? And why should the spring migration be so much more regular and concentrated than the fall one? Why don't I see the same spectacle on the Platte River in September and October that I do in March and April?

I noticed, too, that despite their great numbers, the sandhill cranes do not crowd the roost, as other birds do. They spread out along the river in elongated ovals, in some places no more than a few birds deep, conforming to the shapes of the submerged sandbars.

And why the continuous racket? What message are they conveying? I notice that as the dawn approaches, the intensity of the singing escalates, reaching its peak as the birds take to the air for the day. It sounds nervous, and the closer the daylight is, the more like an incantation of excitement the singing sounds. I think often when I listen to them of the chorus that emerges in the distance from a schoolyard of children at recess. What is the meaning of this constant singing? When the cranes are on the wing, their language is lower, calmer, somehow more functional-sounding. Some biologists have hypothesized that it is a way of keeping in touch with flockmates who are out of sight. But why, on the ground, should one crane need to keep in constant audio contact with another standing two feet away? It is a great puzzle, this singing of birds.

I drove north, homeward, until noon and then stopped for lunch at the Sherman Reservoir near Loup City. I was still deep in the sandhills but worlds away from the cranes on the North Platte. I had left the snow behind. Brilliant sunshine streamed down, but a stiff wind blew, and the air had grown raw and cold. I carried the ice chest to the picnic table, rummaged in it for a sausage and a block of cheese, made myself a sandwich. It was not much of an Easter repast, I had to admit. I had taken only one bite when I heard, as if it were an echo, the crying of cranes. I disregarded it, took another bite. But the sound of cranes came again, clear, unmistakable. Searching the sky, I spotted them high overhead, distinguishable only as specks, sailing on the winds headed north.

I was headed north because my clock and calendar told me I must. I had appointments to keep, business to attend to. I was re-

minded, as I watched the cranes through binoculars, that they have their own internal clocks, as regular and demanding as mine. Even birds hatched and raised in the laboratory, deprived of any experience with migration, cut off from external clues, subjected, for example, to a lifetime succession of days and nights of exactly equal length and unvarying climate, even such birds show a certain anxiety in the spring and fall when their wild brethren are migrating. They pace nervously in the night. In the fall they choose perches on the south sides of their cages, in the spring on the north sides. They molt. They eat more than normal. If released, they take to the air. This behavior, regulated by some genetic timepiece, is called "migratory restlessness." It is, I think, one of the most felicitous terms in the biological literature.

I watched until the cranes disappeared from sight. Buffeted by the wind, I turned toward the car, caught in the throes of my own migratory restlessness. I ached to follow them, to rise up on wings of my own, to fly with them to some wild and unbounded place.

On the radio the next morning I heard reports of the storm in western Nebraska. Eight-foot drifts of snow. Thousands of motorists stranded. Interstate highways closed. All commerce at a standstill. I was glad to be safe at home. The cranes were safe too, I knew. The ancient faith of the cranes, who had set out so blindly a month earlier under a warm southwestern sun into the treacherous northern spring, the ancient faith of the cranes had once again been affirmed.

ASA WRIGHT AND HER TROPICAL FOREST ARK

TEXT BY FRANK GRAHAM JR.

•

PAINTINGS BY ARTHUR SINGER

The crowd of taxi drivers, baggage handlers, and assorted loiterers on the make surged around us as we left customs at Trinidad's Piarco Airport. Even before I could frame a question, one of the men noticed the binocular case hanging from my shoulder and asked, "Asa Wright?"

I nodded, and the problem of finding our driver was on the way to being solved.

"Asa Wright," the man said, turning to the others. Recognition flashed on a dozen faces and the crowd scattered, but not before sending up the call, "Asa Wright!" The words seemed to follow and envelop us, and when we walked out onto the sidewalk other people stared at us and then shouted into the sultry tropical night: "Asa Wright!" "Asa Wright!"

What meaning the cry held for the hangers-on, I couldn't guess. (Did it signify for them some person? A place? Perhaps a tutelary goddess, or cabalistic chant?) At any rate, the magic phrase quickly summoned our driver from a distant part of the terminal. A stocky, pleasant-faced, East Indian man materialized at our side, identified him-

Scarlet ibises and a great egret in Trinidad's coastal Caroni Swamp.

self as a bona fide representative of that charmed entity, the Asa Wright Nature Centre, and in a few moments was driving us toward the rainforest in the mountains of northern Trinidad.

It is easy to see why the words "Asa Wright" reverberate in the Trinidadian consciousness. Every year the Asa Wright Nature Centre lures hundreds of strangers to the island to watch birds, a pastime that most of the locals find utterly incomprehensible. And behind the perplexing institution itself stands the image of the woman for whom it was named. Reminiscences about the imposing Asa Wright, who died in 1971, are beginning to take on the larger-than-life haziness of myth.

A woman, no doubt, of many parts: a generous hostess to visiting naturalists, a resourceful manager who made a go of her plantation when her rum-soaked husband fell by the wayside, a hard-living amazon who is said to have repulsed a would-be rapist by biting off part of his tongue. ("The chap is still around, but he can't talk," an old acquaintance of hers says in support of the tale.)

She comes across in those scraps of reminiscence as a character from one of Somerset Maugham's stories of colonial plantation life in the Malay States, or Ceylon—or Trinidad. But it hardly seems to matter now. What matters is the tract of rainforest Asa Wright helped to make known to the world, and which survives in a land where much of the forest is going fast.

We reached the forest by way of a series of narrow switchbacks that climb the steep mountains from the densely settled lowlands. (Formerly a British crown colony, the island is now part of the Republic of Trinidad and Tobago, off the coast of Venezuela.) The nature center stands at the head of the Arima Valley, flanked by wooded ridges that shorten the hours of sunlight and help to plunge the surrounding forest into early darkness. Not so long ago, a visitor could stand on the balcony and look south down the valley across the nearly endless billows of foliage to a vague shimmer that marked the steamy plains. Today the picture reveals a single flaw, a reddish-brown gap in the green expanse where someone has gouged a gravel quarry.

But the foreground was so intensely alive with color and movement that we seldom looked as far as the quarry after our first few minutes on the veranda. Our little world was embowered by the tropical blossoms in the garden below, the tumultuous growth of flowering shrubs along the walkways, and the

strange foliage of trees that frequently grew to a hundred feet or more all around us.

Against this exotic backdrop moved the birds that have drawn birdwatchers to the nature center for decades. The visitors come individually, or in groups led by professional birders. Others come to learn about the birds and the whole living community in the wet tropics.

We could have spent a full day—and in fact, we did—on the veranda without walking the nature center's several trails to satisfy

our desire to see as many birds as possible. Indeed, it would be difficult to find a better vantage point for birding than Asa Wright's veranda. From first light in the morning, when noisy flocks of orange-winged parrots and crested oropendolas were active, until dusk, when the last of the tanagers and honeycreepers faded away to be replaced at the feeders by fruit-eating bats, there was an endless pageant of winged creatures to sort out and admire.

The intense concentration of birds in view

was not wholly natural, of course. The flowering shrubs attracted such spectacular hummingbirds as the white-chested emerald, the white-necked jacobin, and the tufted coquette. The feeding tables, stocked with oranges and bananas, were visited by a spectacular array of small, colorful birds, including purple honeycreepers, red-legged honeycreepers, violaceous euphonias, and silver-beaked, turquoise, white-lined, blue-gray, and palm tanagers.

There was always a commotion on the

A colony of crested oropendolas above Spring Hill.

veranda when someone detected one of the larger birds of the rainforest beyond the garden. Regular visitors included the collared trogon, channel-billed toucan, scaled pigeon, bare-eyed thrush, squirrel cuckoo, yellow-rumped cacique, rufous-browed peppershrike, black-tailed tityra. Overhead, a raptor—white hawk, double-toothed kite, or ornate hawk-eagle—was often in view.

The Asa Wright Nature Centre and the adjoining research station called Simla have a curiously rich and intermingled past. It is not stretching the truth to say that the story began exactly 150 years ago when Alexander Sprunt, a Scottish merchant, arrived in Trinidad. He was soon in business for himself, trading with planters on the island and

Channel-billed toucans.

others in nearby Venezuela. Sprunt was one of the local businessmen who helped to plan and build the first Presbyterian church in Trinidad.

The Sprunt family later located in the Carolinas and for a time lost touch with Trinidad. (In 1935 the original Sprunt's grandson, Alexander Sprunt Jr., became director of southern sanctuaries for the National Audubon Society, and his great-grandson, Alexander "Sandy" Sprunt IV, is now the society's research director.) But ancestor worship helped to renew the ties. During the 1920s a member of the family visited Trinidad and, learning of the Sprunt connection, carried out some historical research on the part her family had played in the island's

past. Later, she passed on her findings to another of the original Alexander Sprunt's grandsons, Joseph A. Holmes.

Holmes, an engineer working at an oilfield in the isolated forest of eastern Venezuela, welcomed the news of a family connection in Trinidad. The island's capital, Port of Spain, was the most accessible town for the oilfield workers who wanted to shop, carouse, or have a tooth filled. On their frequent trips to Port of Spain, Holmes and his wife, Helen-Bruce, attended Greyfriars, the church of which his grandfather had been a co-founder; they became members of the congregation and arranged to have a tablet inscribed there in his memory.

During one of his trips, Holmes learned

from a couple of scientists about an old coffee and cocoa plantation, Spring Hill, that had been acquired by the government land bank in default of taxes. What especially aroused his interest was a report that Spring Hill was the site of a cave where oilbirds nested. Holmes had visited the cave at Caripe in northern Venezuela where the famous naturalist and traveler Alexander von Humboldt had discovered those rare nocturnal birds for science in 1799. The few known oilbird colonies had always been located in remote caves, deep in the jungle or high above the sea. The cave at Spring Hill was probably the most accessible nesting site in the world.

Joseph and Helen-Bruce Holmes bought Spring Hill in 1936. She spent more time there than her husband did, because he was tied to his engineering duties on the mainland and, later, to the U.S. Army during World War II. Joined by her parents, she directed much of the renovation of the main building, the replanting of the gardens, and the clearing of underbrush around the coffee and cocoa trees. (During the latter operation, workers killed some fifty bushmasters, among the deadliest snakes in the American tropics but not likely to be encountered on the grounds today.) Helen-Bruce also created a forest bathing pool at the foot of a waterfall.

Holmes later referred to the plantation as "a garden of Eden," a phrase echoed since then by visitors to the area. But after the war the Holmeses began spending more of their time in the United States with a view toward retirement, and the plantation suffered under local overseers. Holmes recalled the old planters' expression that "cocoa grows best within the sound of the owner's voice."

At this point Asa Wright entered the picture. She was a large, handsome woman, the daughter of an Icelandic surgeon and diplomat. (The pronunciation of her first name in Icelandic sounds something like "Ow-sa," though most people connected with the nature center say "Ah-sa.") When she and her British husband, Newcombe Wright, a sometime lawyer and civil servant, arrived in Trinidad they became acquainted with the Holmeses; eventually they bought Spring Hill.

Although the Wrights' announced aim in buying the property was to keep it going as a profitable plantation, Newcombe apparently saw it as a rest home where he would build up his fragile health. Old-timers remember him slinging a hammock, putting a tray with an ice-filled glass and a bottle of rum close at hand, and spending the day in boozy indolence. Asa threw herself into the day-to-day management of the plantation. Eric Patience, for some years director of civil aviation in Trinidad and Tobago and later the nature center's director, recalls his first meeting with her.

"I was in a grocery store, talking to the manager, when Asa Wright walked in carrying a large sack of vegetables on her shoulder," Patience says. "She threw the sack on the counter and said, 'Here's some vegetables for you to buy.' She wasn't selling them, you understand. The store owner was buying them."

At about the same time the Wrights bought Spring Hill, an eminent scientist became their neighbor. William Beebe of the New York Zoological Society, who was one of the foremost authorities on the New World's tropics, had been looking for a suitable area of rainforest which he could use as a permanent headquarters for his various projects. He found the ideal property adjoining Spring Hill—twenty-two acres of virgin forest on which the colonial government had built a large house at the turn of the century as a potential country residence for the island's governor. The house had been named Simla, after the old summer capital of the British in the hills of northern India.

Although no governors of Trinidad had made use of the estate, the long, low, hilltop building, built of cedar planks with an asbestos roof and jalousied sides, suited Beebe's purpose. He bought the property and turned it over to the New York Zoological Society for its Department of Tropical Research. Soon he was joined there by a procession of scientists carrying on their studies of the rainforest's flora and fauna.

A chief attraction for many of those scientists was the cave-like chasm carved from bedrock by a stream running through Spring Hill, the site of the famous oilbird colony. Asa Wright became the center of the scientific community's social life. She took a keen interest in the scientists' work and threw open her house to them. One of her visitors was the British ornithologist David Snow, who studied the resident oilbirds for more than four years.

"I shall never forget the kindness and hospitality of Asa Wright, and how she welcomed me and regaled me with tea and chocolate cake after I returned from my inspection of the nests," Snow wrote later.

Another frequent visitor was John Dunston, an entomologist and Trinidad resident who volunteered to help at both Simla and Spring Hill. He protected the oilbirds from local poachers, who found the plump young birds especially good eating. (There is no record of Trinidadians boiling down the

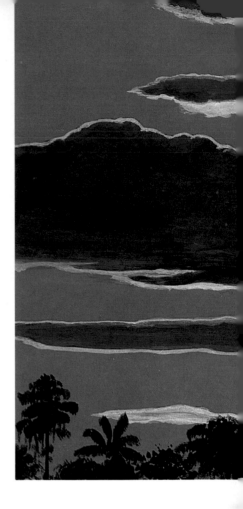

An oilbird feeding on palm nuts by moonlight.

young birds for their fat, as was the custom in nearby Venezuela.) Dunston also built an artificial nest ledge in the cave to increase nesting space, and when he died in 1972 the cave was named in his memory.

Oilbirds are unique. Although related to the whippoorwills and nightjars, they live in a taxonomic family of their own, Steatornithidae. They are about eighteen inches long, with a wingspan of more than three feet and dark brown plumage spotted with white. Like some large form of bat, they remain in their caves during the day and find their way about in the dimness there by emitting a series of audible clicks for echolocation. They emerge at night to roam the forest in search of ripe fruit, which they apparently find by their well-developed sense of smell and wrench from trees with their strong hooked beaks.

David Snow, who studied the oilbirds at Spring Hill, resolved a number of aspects of their natural history that had long puzzled ornithologists. He discovered, for instance, that the average age of young birds leaving the nest was nearly 110 days, a nestling period that is approached only by some of the larger seabirds and birds of prey. The extreme fatness of the young, he speculates, is a consequence of the fat content of the fruit fed to them by the adults, and which cannot

be burned up during the chick's long period of inactivity.

"It may be useful at this stage, in conjunction with the nestling's thick coat of down, in providing insulation in the comparatively cool conditions of the caves," Snow wrote. "Later, as the young become more active and the feathers begin to grow, the fat is used up, until the young bird fledges at about the same weight as the adult. It may be that the speed with which the accumulated fat can be used up is another factor affecting the length of time that the young remain in the nest."

The colonial habits of oilbirds and the unique adaptations during the breeding cycle are, as Snow discovered, a direct result of the changeover by some remote ancestral nightjar from eating insects to eating fruit. The research Snow carried out on a variety of forest birds at Simla and Spring Hill, often with his wife, Barbara, provided much of the material for his book *The Web of Adaptation.* One of the classics of bird studies in the tropics, it is essentially an investigation into the evolutionary consequences of a bird's depending on fruit for much or all of its diet.

Insects, as Snow pointed out in his book, "don't want to be eaten." They have evolved an incredible diversity of means to avoid detection and capture, while birds, to keep up with these defensive strategies, have evolved

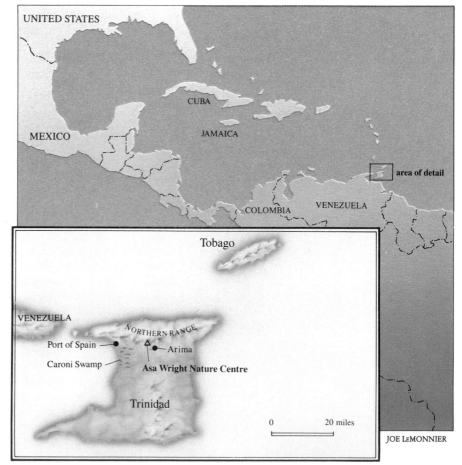

JOE LeMONNIER

comparatively diverse characteristics to aid in capturing them. The abundance of avian adaptations to insect defenses helps to account for the bewildering number of insect-eating birds in the tropics. But, even though they are equipped to function as predators on insects, these birds must spend most of their time hunting their "wily" prey.

"Fruit 'wants' to be eaten," Snow wrote. "The more of it that the plant produces, and the more attractive it makes its fruit, the more widely will its seeds be dispersed and the more likely it will be to propagate itself. And so such fruit tends to be abundant and conspicuous, and a fruit-eating bird may need to devote a very short period each day to foraging."

Like some favored courtier, then, tropical fruit-eating birds enjoy abundant leisure and occupy themselves in dalliance. The males have evolved extravagant physical characteristics—plumes or crests or wattles, enormous beaks or gaudy patches of bare skin— and elaborate displays in order to surpass their rivals for the females' attention.

The spectacular evidence of this evolutionary explosion, displayed here on the forest's edges and along the valley's trails, drew the attention of scientists and bird-watchers from all over Europe and North America. Spring Hill, with its wealth of birds and ease of access to the forest, began to win an international reputation. So, it seems, did its chatelaine. When Newcombe Wright died, Asa sought permission from the authorities to have him buried on the plantation, but she was turned down on the basis that burial could take place only in an approved cemetery.

"It just happened that John Dunston stopped at Spring Hill about a week after Newcombe died," says Eric Patience. "He guessed something was wrong, looked around the place, and discovered Newcombe's body laid out on a table in one of the cottages—it's now room seven. Asa apparently had got her back up about the authorities and wasn't going to give in. After seven days in this tropical climate, poor Newcombe was quite ripe."

Dunston rushed to Port of Spain and returned with a coffin and a quantity of ice, into which he had the body properly packed. Meanwhile, word of Asa's bereavement had spread through the island, and dozens of friends appeared to pay their respects. Soon an old-fashioned wake was in progress, with Asa taking her share of the libation. By late evening, ice for the drinks was running low.

"Asa, do you think that Newcombe would mind if we borrowed some of his ice?" one of the mourners asked.

"Not at all, dear," Asa replied. "Go right ahead."

And the remains were once more left to the ravages of the climate.

As time went on, Asa Wright accommodated the overflow of visiting scientists at Simla as well as naturalists and illustrators who wanted to view the forest and its inhabitants at Spring Hill. (Don Eckelberry painted many of his most famous bird portraits on the grounds.) But plantation labor was hard to come by, and it was obvious that Asa Wright faced dwindling physical and financial resources.

The regulars at Spring Hill knew they had to act quickly to avert a catastrophe. Logging was going on in the hills around the plantation, and with William Beebe dead, Simla itself fell on hard times. In 1967 Erma Fisk, a prominent ornithologist and conservationist, joined with Eckelberry, Russell Mason (of Florida Audubon Society), and others to raise money to buy the estate.

The Asa Wright Nature Centre was established with its own board of directors, composed of eleven Trinidadians and ten foreigners from the United States, Canada, Great Britain, and elsewhere. Asa Wright remained there until her death in 1971. A few years later the New York Zoological Society surrendered its interest in Simla, and the research station became part of the nature center.

The importance to Trinidad of this private

nature reserve increases with time. As in most tropical nations, birds face the twin hazards of forest destruction and indiscriminate shooting, with only halfhearted protection by the government. Neglect is not solely a matter of ignorance: Every currency note issued by the government bears the country's coat of arms, the chief components of which are illustrations of the national bird of Trinidad, the scarlet ibis, and that of Tobago, the rufous-vented chachalaca (or "cocrico," a bird as conspicuous for its raucous call as the scarlet ibis is for its striking plumage). Both are frequent victims of poachers.

A major problem area in Trinidad right now is the Caroni Swamp, forty square miles of mangroves and nutrient-rich shallows which form a haven for more than 160 species of birds. Before the British gave up Trinidad and Tobago, they established a bird sanctuary in the heart of the swamp, chiefly for the protection of the scarlet ibis. Every visitor to the Asa Wright Nature Centre eventually arranges for a trip into this huge swamp on Trinidad's western coast.

We went, as most birdwatchers do, in the boat operated by a knowledgeable and articulate local ornithologist named Winston Nanan. In late afternoon, as we were about to leave the dock, our departure was delayed for a few minutes by a string of small boats coming out of the narrow waterway through the mangroves. Standing in the bow of the lead boat, brandishing a shotgun in one hand and waving to acquaintances on the shore with the other, was a man Nanan identified as a high government official.

"He and his friends have been hunting in the swamp," Nanan said. "He likes to eat ibis."

On the way into the swamp, Nanan explained the complexity of the mangrove ecosystem and its associated mudbars and shallows. He indicated the varieties of fiddler crabs, important food for ibises and other birds and so numerous that the mudbanks themselves seemed to be in a continual flutter. Foureye fish scuttled through the shallows on rapidly beating fins, their peculiar eyes divided into segments that enable them to see prey underwater while keeping watch for potential predators in that lighter element, the air. Overhead, a pretty little bat falcon cruised idly, waiting for what the dusk had to offer.

Nanan tied his boat to a mangrove limb and painstakingly pointed out to those aboard a common potoo, a bird about fifteen inches long that, when at rest, is practically indistinguishable from the stump to which it clings. It is simply a bulge in the trunk, an excrescence of mottled bark. We passengers accepted Nanan's identification on faith.

Then a cry of "Ibises!" went up. A spatter of the purest red swept across the early evening sky. It was followed by another, and another. We trailed those fugitive glints down the waterway, rounded a bend, and found directly in front of us the scene we had come thousands of miles to see. A gentle sigh, part awe and part disbelief, escaped us in unison.

The arrival of the scarlet ibises at their roosting place in the mangroves is the most spectacular exhibition in the avian world. Repeat: The arrival of the scarlet ibises at their roosting place in the mangroves is the most spectacular exhibition in the avian world. If you hear a report of any other contender for that honor, dismiss it at once. There are gatherings of birds more overwhelming in their numbers, diversity, general uproar, or in the sublimity of their setting, but none that equals the stunning vision of these outrageously colored birds as they settle by the hundreds at dusk into the dark green leaves of the swamp.

The declining sun seems to draw out and concentrate all the color on the surface of their plumage, so that the birds appear almost two-dimensional. No picture or essay conveys the richness of that sheen of scarlet against foliage. A superb painter or photographer can come back from the Caroni Swamp with a realistic portrait of the scene. Only the human eye registers its unreality.

Estimates of the scarlet ibis population in Trinidad vary, probably because the actual numbers also fluctuate. Parts of the population are constantly in transit between Trinidad and the South American mainland. Winston Nanan thinks there are 13,000 to 15,000 individuals on the island at present, but ornithologists generally agree that the number now actually nesting in the Caroni Swamp is very small.

"Ten or twelve years ago the poaching reached a peak here when the ibis colony was shot out during the breeding season," Nanan told us. "After that, the nesting on Trinidad was disrupted. Some birds began to nest in the fall, and others abandoned the swamp and began nesting in the Orinoco Delta over on the mainland."

The fragility of nesting patterns was brought home to us again a few days later at the Asa Wright Nature Centre. Although the oilbird cave is only a ten-minute walk from the main house and has been strictly protected for some years, the breeding colony fluctuates. Have the birds been loved to excess by their visiting admirers? David Snow

reported that his almost daily visits to the cave more than a quarter of a century ago seemed to have no effect on the oilbirds' routine, so that he could often put a ladder against a nesting ledge and climb up to examine the chicks without frightening the parent bird from the nest.

But something is making the cave uncomfortable for the oilbirds, and Rita Iton, the center's new director, has restricted access to the colony. The week before our arrival at the nature center, only two birds and no nests had been found in the cave. Although there is another well-known oilbird colony on Trinidad, it would be a catastrophe of sorts to lose the one at this historic and accessible site.

One morning after a rain, an old man, the nature center's guide to Dunston Cave, came for us. We followed him into the forest. The smell of damp earth and the warm exhalations of soggy plants would be familiar to every frequenter of greenhouses. Golden-headed manakins were points of yellow fire in the forest gloom. A bearded bellbird's deliberate *tok! tok! tok!* reverberated like a carpenter's hammerblows in a shut-up house.

The old man eased his way with a walking stick down the steep path. In this place, a tributary of the Arima River has sliced through the rock, creating a "cave" that is really a narrow fissure partly roofed and tilted downward in a series of low waterfalls. Not even the din made by the torrent blotted out the bellbird's explosive chant.

We descended the most abrupt of the waterfalls by balancing ourselves gingerly on a metal ladder that served as a ramp. The light was faint in the tunnel, but we could see well enough to know that the nest ledges a dozen or so feet above us were deserted. The oilbirds had flown, deepening the cave's mystery. (Happily, they returned after some weeks, perhaps having made their point about not being pushed too hard. The cave itself has now been put off limits to human visitors, though the birds can easily be observed from the streambed outside.)

After leaving the cave that day, I walked on alone into the forest, in pursuit of that insistent yet ventriloquial call of the bellbird. But it's hard to stay single-minded in the rainforest. Distractions abound. A pair of barred antshrikes uttered their clucking notes in concert and showed themselves at the forest edge—small but striking birds with sporty crests, the male looking faintly comical in his black-and-white-striped plumage, like a cartoon convict, and the remarkably handsome female in buffs and rich chestnut-browns.

A familiar note set me up for a pleasant surprise. There on the forest floor, a transient

A pair of white-tailed trogons.

Bearded bellbird.

among the alien corn, as it were, bobbed a northern waterthrush, a bird I had always associated with New England streamsides. I found this tropical forest, in fact, winter home to a number of species we tend to think of as northern natives. Prominent among them was the American redstart, which *really* looked at home in the rainforest, the male in its black and orange-red plumage outshining most of the resident birds with which it consorted.

A series of sharp reports, like little firecrackers detonating in the understory, lured me off the trail to what proved to be a lek, or courting ground, of the white-bearded manakin. The male suggests an obese black-capped chickadee, a round ball of fluff, with its head appearing only as a slight protuberance at one point on the sphere and hardly noticeable in the mass of enveloping feathers.

Like most of the other local fruit-eaters, the males seem to have little to do but hang out. They frequent the lek, a small clearing in the forest, where they perform an intricate series of displays in the hope of securing the attention of any females (rather drab, greenish birds) that happen by. The males make use of saplings and small trees as courting stations. They practically bounce off the trunks as they flit from one to another, low over the ground, performing a succession of midair acrobatics, puffing up their snowy throat feathers (or "beards"), and setting off those surprisingly loud percussions by a lightning snap of their wings. A lek is where the action is.

I felt as a child must on a visit to Disneyland. One long-cherished fantasy after another appeared for a moment before my eyes and then faded again into the forest shadows. My passion for tropical birds had been aroused nearly a quarter of a century earlier when I first saw Arthur Singer's paintings of trogons in Oliver Austin's *Birds of the World*. Birds, I felt at that moment, surely breathed a rarer atmosphere than mere mortals.

Now, perched stolidly on a limb close by and framed in green filigree, was a white-tailed trogon. Its golden-yellow breast, even its green back, shone like metal in a stray shaft of sunlight.

A little farther along, a soft hooting note attracted me to another bird, which (through paintings looked at, and looked at again) already seemed a familiar species. It was a

White-bearded manakins.

blue-crowned motmot. The blue head and tail, rich green back, and rufous chest and belly reminded me that the alternative vernacular name, blue-diademed motmot—favored by ornithologists such as Alexander Skutch—celebrates more aptly the fanciful elegance of this forest bird.

And at last there was a splendid view through binoculars of a bearded bellbird. It sat perfectly still, high in a tree over the path—a stocky, jay-sized bird, with a pale-gray body (looking white at a distance), black wings, and a brown head. Hanging from its short, broad beak was a dark, stringy mass of wattles, giving the bird at rest a vague resemblance to the bearded villain in an old Russian movie. Rasputin, born again in a happier guise!

And suddenly the bird was gone, rising higher into the forest canopy to resume sounding what is probably the loudest of all bird calls. David and Barbara Snow, who studied the bearded bellbird at Spring Hill, compared its two slightly varying calls to a hammer striking a block of wood. They are not as resonant as the bell-like note of its close relative, the white bellbird, which gives the family its name.

"At least two years of learning may be needed before the fully adult calls are mastered," David Snow wrote of the bearded bellbird, "and the presence of calling adults is almost certainly a necessary condition for learning the normal calls of the species."

But when they studied this species in Venezuela, the Snows discovered a revealing fact. The mainland birds uttered a third note, quite bell-like, which the American ornithologists William Brewster and Frank M. Chapman, visiting Trinidad in 1893, had also described. This musical call is never heard on the island today.

"Probably at some time in the past the bellbirds of the Northern Range [of Trinidad] were much reduced in numbers so that there were not enough adult males to pass on the tradition," Snow wrote in *The Web of Adaptation.* "It may be significant that the element which has been lost is the most complex, and thus the one which would be expected to take the longest to learn."

A curious sort of extinction, a call evolved over the centuries and then snuffed out in a matter of years. A gap in the racial memory. The forest ark that Asa Wright handed on already harbors its share of ghosts.

BUTCHERBIRD

PHOTOGRAPHY BY TOM J. ULRICH

A predatory songbird without talons, the loggerhead shrike earned such an unflattering nickname for its characteristic habit of impaling victims—mice, small birds, and insects—on thorns, twigs, or barbed wire before tearing them apart with its hooked beak. This robin-sized inhabitant of grasslands, orchards, and deserts from southern Canada to Florida and Mexico has a head unusually large in proportion to its body, hence the name "loggerhead."

WINDBIRDS
BY THE BAY

PHOTOGRAPHY BY THOMAS D. ROUNTREE

Above: Sanderling
Right: Dunlin

Left: American Avocet
Above: Western Sandpiper

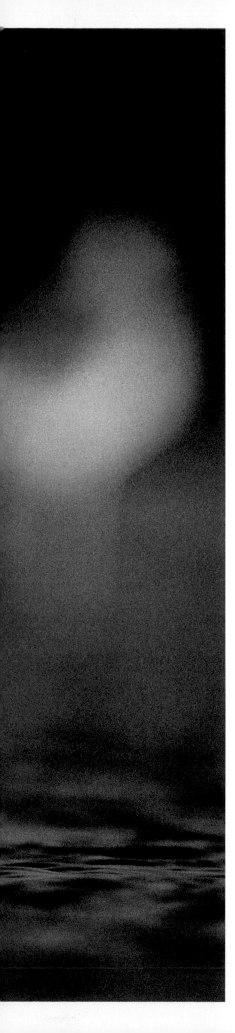

Left: Greater Yellowlegs
Above: Long-Billed Dowitcher

Above: Willet
Right: Black-Necked Stilt

III
NATURAL PHENOMENA

GREAT EGRET AND LOBLOLLY PINE, CHINCOTEAGUE NATIONAL WILDLIFE REFUGE, VIRGINIA BY GLENN VAN NIMWEGEN

OUR WORLD
BY FOG TRANSFORMED

*Sunrise over pond,
Roscommon County,
Michigan (Bruce
Matheson).*

*Cattails and reeds in
pond, Roscommon
County, Michigan
(John Shaw).*

Sawgrass and hammocks at dawn, Everglades National Park, Florida (Glenn Van Nimwegen).

Snow geese and salt marsh, Brigantine National Wildlife Refuge, New Jersey (Glenn Van Nimwegen).

Great egret in freshwater marsh, Brigantine Refuge (Glenn Van Nimwegen).

Wood ducks, De Soto National Wildlife Refuge, Iowa (John Shaw).

Great blue heron rooker Orange, Massachusetts (Mark Picard).

Western redcedar, hemlock, and alder, Snohomish River Valley, Washington (Art Wolfe).

Mating moose, Denali National Park, Alaska (Michio Hoshino/Animals & Earth photo).

*Fogbank, Machias B[...]
Maine (Joe Devenney[...]
Image Bank).*

*Rhodora and lichen-
covered granite, Acadia
National Park, Maine
(Glenn Van Nimwegen).*

THE STUFF OF DREAMS AND DREAD

TEXT BY FRANK GRAHAM JR.

North Head Lighthouse, near the mouth of the Columbia River, Washington (Ray Atkson). Previous page: Golden Gate Bridge, San Francisco, California (Craig Aurness/Westlight).

I am a deep sleeper, not likely to be roused by the sharp little creaks or clangs of the dark that seem to fracture a night's rest for others. But some quality of insistence, part physical, part the stuff of old dreams, may get to me after midnight. No other sound consistently reaches so far down into my sleep and brings me back to the moment as the hoarse, repetitive notes that filter through—from ten miles away—when there is a faint breeze from the southwest and the foghorn sounds at the Petit Manan Lighthouse.

A foghorn, like a gull's cry and the thunder that waves make on a distant beach, is the music of the sea for most of us with a romantic turn of mind. The true mariner, of course, goes beyond those marks of the littoral into the ocean's heart. There, one's ship is the source of nearly all sound. A ship snatches remote voices from the air in its wires and serves as a sounding board for winds and waves. But a foghorn speaks of the menace that lies at the edge of land, calling up thoughts of heroism or penetrating the night to disturb our dreams.

The most ardent admirer of wild nature is unlikely to talk of *loving* fog, as he might love sunshine or snow. Fog is too flimsy a stuff, too like *nothing,* though it functions with all the solidity of a veil and leaves on whatever it touches a thin smear of the moisture that is its substance. It is, as a scientist writes, "a great swarmlike assemblage in the surface air of hundreds of thousands of droplets per cubic inch so minute that it would take seven billion of them to make a teaspoonful of water." But in what it clothes, and in what it reveals, fog transforms our world, gilds it in gray, makes the poet in each of us wonder again at the variety of masks that nature puts on and off to enchant us.

It was in fog that I first saw the part of Maine's coast where I have made my home for more than a quarter-century—fog was part of the enchantment that caught and held me. We drove down a peninsula on a narrow dirt road along which the spruces dripped with old-man's-beard lichen and moisture pilfered from the dense vapor. The landscape was ghostly, and the drive seemed endless. At last our prospective landlords stopped at a small cove and we got out and stood there, looking into the fog.

It had receded somewhat, baring an indeterminate stretch of mudflat. There was no water in sight, but we were assured it was out there someplace in the murk. The stillness was profound. No leaf rustled, no bird cried. We stared at this shrouded seascape as if it held some exalting and momentous revelation. For the moment it made us no overture. The sea and the fog were not ready to grant these newcomers their blessing.

But as we chatted on the shore, unwilling to commit ourselves to this new place, the elements conspired to force our hand. A breeze came up, stirring and tearing the fog, and the water came into view a long way out across the mud. It was simply a glint at first, like a puddle creeping under a door. Then it gained substance. We became aware of an impending event outside our previous experience. The breeze was out of the south, and it seemed to push the water ahead of it under the fog, urging it nearer, amplifying the sense of primal movement with a low soughing that sounded like a thousand people whispering "chrysalises."

The sea's sudden appearance out of the fog, its surface agitated by the light wind, gave it an extraordinary illusion of velocity. That it was two hours or more before the tide finally pushed its foaming front edge up the narrow sand beach where we stood did not alter that impression. It was a time in my life when I was opening myself as never before to the various experiences of the natural world. To dwell in its active presence was to nourish one's sense of being alive. Here the inexorable rhythm of the tides combined with that vaporous broth, the fog, to make manifest the force of sun and moon and Earth's endless spinning on this wild coast. It was a recurring drama I would find hard to leave behind.

Much has changed since my first day on this coast, but not the tides and fogs. A hasty glance at the tide chart tells me when the sea comes and goes, though the fog keeps to no timetable (a statement a visitor might not accept in July, when our planned outings are canceled morning after morning as the fog closes in). But often by day I can see a thick fogbank hovering just offshore. As it begins to move up the bay, one island after another is doused like a flame under an old-fashioned candle-snuffer, and soon the murk

is all around me, with the trees dripping. If I can hear the horn at Petit Manan, the atmosphere seems denser still.

There has been a lighthouse on Petit Manan, a treeless island of nine acres, since 1817. It was built by the federal government to mark a treacherous reef that runs to the island from a point of the same name a couple of miles away. Apparently the original tower was a sorry affair, already crumbling when a government inspector stopped there fourteen years later. The lightkeeper's dwelling was leaking badly, and the dispirited keeper had long since fled to the mainland. The fellow's wife, built of sterner stuff, had taken over for him.

In due course a more reliable keeper was found. (The poor wife, citing experience, applied for the job after her husband's death but, predictably, was turned down by the male authorities.) And in 1855 a new granite lighthouse went up. Although the tower was 119 feet high, one of the tallest on the Atlantic Coast, it was recognized that a warning light alone was not enough to keep a passing ship off the rocks. How could mariners be alerted in dense fog?

E. Price Edwards, a historian of British lighthouses writing over a century ago, mentioned his own country's attempts to grapple with the problem:

"It is proper, however, to observe that the lighthouse authorities in the United States took up the matter practically before it engaged much consideration in this country, owing to the East Coast of America being in an exceptionable degree liable to the visitation of fog, by which the coasting traffic was seriously inconvenienced; and the necessity arose for something to be done whereby the difficulty might be obviated. The ready genius of the country was not long in coming to conclusions, and although some kinds of sound signals, such as bells, gongs, etc., were employed in Europe, the Americans first brought into use Brobdignagian trumpets, whistles, etc."

So even before the disintegrating tower came down at Petit Manan Island, the government installed one of the newfangled fog signal bells there. Edward Rowe Snow, in *The Lighthouses of New England,* has described the next step in the struggle against the hazards of fog in our area, which was the placing of a foghorn at the lighthouse in 1869:

"The water supply for the fog steam signal created quite a problem, however, for a nearby swamp was found to contain too much vegetable matter. Finally the old keeper's dwelling was roofed over and fitted with gutters, which carried rainwater into two wooden tanks in the cellar. Pipes ran from the cellar to the fog signal station, and the water problem was solved."

The electrical age brought refinements to the signals. At last technology made even lighthouse keepers obsolete. They were taken off Petit Manan in 1972, and the station became fully automated. Now machines are in charge, keeping the light flashing and sending the recurrent deep moan out through the gloom.

In summer the island is a welter of stench and shriek—the result of one of the few large tern colonies surviving on the Maine coast. Fog shows its baleful aspect then. Herring gulls, which nest just across a narrow bar on Green Island, ordinarily forage for miles around during the day but may change their habits when the fog rolls in. Then, like yachtsmen or bathers, they tend to wait it out. They concentrate on the nesting terns conveniently close at hand, gliding in on their nests in the poor visibility, and there is a rise in the predation of eggs and chicks.

But on the mainland, summer fogs bring unexpected pleasures to stay-at-home humans. Wildflowers, their colors sometimes bleached out under a bright sun, acquire an extraordinary luminosity against the pallid backdrop. Birdsong takes on a haunting quality missing on fine days. The flute-like notes of the hermit thrush, exquisite under any conditions, seem to come from another world as day fades into dusk or mist, and we hear again the chant that Whitman recalled in another kind of gloom in "When Lilacs Last in the Dooryard Bloom'd":

Sing on, sing on you gray-brown bird,
Sing from the swamps, the recesses,
   pour your chant from the bushes,
Limitless out of the dusk, out of the
   cedars and pines.

Still, if I had one bird to choose as the voice of the fog in the northern forest, it would be the white-throated sparrow. Friends of mine on the coast who knew the dreamy song but not the name of the singer always called it "the Beethoven bird." After listening to it as it sang in the alders one foggy June evening, I hesitated to tell them its "real" name for fear of breaking a fragile spell.

We think of fog as a veil, hiding or distorting reality. But when I walk out into a morning when all the world beyond the nearest meadow is blotted out, I find another world brought into focus right at my feet. In June every bush glistens with the layered webs of the bowl and doily spiders, convex

meshes suspended between twigs with another broad horizontal web below, like that stretched for a high-wire artist. As summer matures, the droplets of fog touch up in astonishing detail other webs that go all but unnoticed in bright sunlight—the orbs of the garden spider, the jewel-studded nets of the cobweb weavers enclosing the tips of goldenrod, and the bright rectangles of gossamer in the grass that betray the funnel weavers. The baubles hung on each strand seem to draw the menace from them, and perhaps they do. Are flying insects warned away by all this radiance?

Let the field entomologist handle that question. The one that begs to be answered here is, What is fog? For the poet Carl Sandburg it was simply something that "comes on little cat feet." For the etymologist, it is a word of obscure origin that apparently drifted into modern English from the Scandinavian mists. For the meteorologist, it is a vapor that restricts visibility in any direction to less than one kilometer (0.62 miles). And for the curious of every persuasion, it is a cloud that hugs the ground.

"Whenever the air is cooled, by any means whatever, below its dewpoint, a portion of the water vapor present separates out on such dust particles or other condensation nuclei as happen to be present," wrote the meteorologist W. J. Humphreys in his book *Fogs and Clouds*. "If this process occurs only at a considerable distance above the surface of the Earth, leaving the lower air clear, the result is some form of cloud. If, on the other hand, it extends quite to, or occurs at, the surface of the Earth it is then called a fog, no matter how shallow or how deep it may be. The distinction, therefore, between fog and cloud is that of position. Fog is a cloud on the Earth; a cloud, a fog in the sky."

Let's back up for a moment and review a couple of the necessary elements. Air, to produce fog, must be cooled to its "dewpoint," which means its temperature must fall to the point at which the moisture it holds will condense as dew. And air must hold, in addition to sufficient moisture, minute particles of dust or sea salt. (Most air, of course, holds such solid particles, though air found in deep caves is free of them—fog cannot occur there unless particles are brought in from outside!)

Once you have seen one fog, you *haven't* seen them all. Place and circumstance create fogs that are as different from each other as are those loftier fogs we call clouds. Here follows a variety of recipes for "pea soup."

"Radiation fog" over much of the United States tends to be a product particularly of

Scallop dragger tied at wharf, Yarmouth, Nova Scotia (Stephen Homer).

fall. Months of sunlight have warmed the land and its surface waters, and winter's harsh winds aren't there to blow any mist away. Moisture has been taken up by the lower air through evaporation. The right conditions occur when the weather is clear and still, at night or just before sunrise. At these times a lack of cloud cover allows heat to escape from the surface by radiation and a lack of wind keeps the humid, lower air from mixing with drier, upper air.

On contact with the chilled surface of the land, the saturated air quickly falls to its dewpoint. Its water vapor condenses into droplets around the solid particles present in the air. The resulting fog is usually brief, burning off when the sun heats the land again later in the morning.

"Upslope fog" forms on the lee side of hills and mountains and can be a spectacular sight on the eastern slopes of the Rockies. Warm air, let's say from the Gulf of Mexico, moves across the Great Plains and reaches the Rockies. As the air rises up the slopes it spreads and cools, though *without* losing heat. (The scientists' phrase for this phenom-

enon is "adiabatic cooling," as the cooling is simply a result of decreased pressure within the air mass.) As the dewpoint is reached, fog forms—great swirling billows that may look like "clouds" to an observer far below but are certainly fog to anyone stranded in them. As the air rises over the ridges and begins its descent on the western slopes, pressure rekindles its heat and the fog dissipates.

"Sea smoke" summons visions of Arctic shores, and that's where it is likely to be seen. Wintry air, slowly moving from a land mass like that of Labrador or northern Russia, passes over nearby coastal seas that are comparatively warm. Surface water evaporates into the cold air, saturating it so that ice crystals begin to form and produce fog. No fog will develop, however, if the cold air arrives on strong winds that scatter the water vapor so widely that it never completely saturates the air.

Researchers report that true sea smoke sometimes appears well south of Arctic waters. "I remember coming out on deck on the old research vessel *Crawford* one winter morning and finding not only a sea smoke

101

Gathering dulse, Grand Manan Island, New Brunswick (Stephen Homer photo)

suddenly arrives over colder inshore water. People far inland also know this kind of fog, especially after fall nights when air from more southerly places stagnates over the rapidly cooling land. But advection fog has become part of the local lore and legend of places redolent of the sea, including San Francisco, the Maine coast, and the fishing banks off Newfoundland.

"Advection" is defined as the horizontal movement of a mass of air which alters the air's temperature and other physical properties. This fog gives San Francisco its damp chill—or "natural air-conditioning," as the natives like to say—and they go on to brag about it in the very way that a Miami Beach hotel operator might extol the local sun. The air itself comes from far out in the balmy Pacific. Approaching the coast, it crosses a band of cold, upwelling inshore water (similar to that off Chile), and presto, the clear air of the tropical islands turns mean and gray.

And intensely picturesque, if you are susceptible to that sort of thing. In summer it pours in past the Golden Gate Bridge, wreathing it in enormous vapory tendrils and sometimes smothering it altogether. (It is said that thick fog may have been the reason that Sir Francis Drake missed San Francisco Bay completely when he came down the coast in his square rigger, *Golden Hind,* more than four centuries ago. He anchored in the lee of nearby Point Reyes and landed on the Farallon Islands, thirty-two miles west of the bay.) Drifting past the bridge, the fog covers the bay, setting off various foghorns that have long since replaced the cannon placed at Point Bonita in the 1850s and fired every half-hour to warn fogbound ships away from the rocks. The fog then blankets parts of the great city around the bay, causing cops and cable car drivers to don bright yellow slickers.

Although local variations in topography, ocean currents, and weather patterns breed for the experts almost as many kinds of fogs as there are beetles for the entomologists, the sharp-eyed observer can pick up similarities when shifting from coast to coast. The horizontal movement from warm ocean to colder inshore water that we find off California has its counterpart in the Atlantic because of the Gulf Stream, that great "river in the sea" that is a mile deep and about ninety-five miles wide. Rachel Carson, in *The Sea Around Us,* described its flow northward from the tropics:

"Beyond Hatteras, the Stream leaves the [continental] shelf, turning northeastward, as a narrow, meandering current, always sharply separated from the water on either

fog but the ship's entire deck and superstructure covered with inches of hard frost rime," Nicholas C. Rosa wrote in the magazine *Oceans.* "We were northward and homeward bound, about a day away from Woods Hole, Massachusetts, still south of latitude 40 degrees and still in Gulf Stream water. But on some recent day a cold front had swept far off the land, dragging a dome of true Arctic air with it; the air temperature at sea was well below freezing, and back at Woods Hole, below zero Fahrenheit. Most of the crew were on deck with shovels and other tools, banging and chopping to get rid of the stuff."

Landlubbers can view a fog similar to sea smoke when lakes and rivers begin to "steam" on frosty mornings. Again, the fog is caused by cold air from the land drifting slowly across warmer water.

"Advection fog" is familiar to anyone who lives on the Atlantic or Pacific coasts of North America. Its origin is the same on either shore—it occurs in air that has picked up moisture over warm, even tropical, seas and side. Off the 'tail' of the Grand Banks the line is most sharply drawn between the cold, bottle-green Arctic water of the Labrador Current and the warm indigo blue of the Stream. In winter the temperature change across the current boundary is so abrupt that as a ship crosses into the Gulf Stream her bow may be momentarily in water 20 degrees warmer than that at her stern, as though the 'cold wall' were a solid barrier separating the two water masses. One of the densest fog-banks in the world lies in this region over the cold water of the Labrador Current—a thick, blanketing whiteness that is the atmospheric response to the Gulf Stream's invasion of the cold northern seas.''

This region of all-embracing advection fogs was made memorable for many of us by Rudyard Kipling in *Captains Courageous* (and its film version with Spencer Tracy as the Portuguese fisherman). There, for days on end, the snippy little kid who fell over-board from an ocean liner works beside his new friend, Manuel, in the "curdly, glidy fog banks,'' while the fisherman blows his big conch-shell horn into the mists to signal his whereabouts to passing vessels. Tragedy strikes "while sea and sky were all milled up in milky fog,'' and a liner runs down one of the little fishing boats.

Along the Maine coast fog has remained part of the lives of people in the fishing villages, as well as those of summer visitors. Samuel Eliot Morison, the well-known historian of the sea, recalled his boyhood vacation trips to Mount Desert Island in the 1890s aboard the old steamboat *City of Richmond*. In his little book *The Story of Mount Desert Island*, Morison wrote:

"She was owned by her skipper, Captain Charles Deering, who carried no insurance and in a thick fog was wont to anchor, while his competitors felt their way along by listening to sheep blatting on the rocky islands, or by the echoes of their own steam whistles. On one occasion, when the *City of Richmond* had anchored for a long time, a passenger inquired of Captain Deering, 'Aren't you going on?' 'Nope.' 'Why not? It's all clear overhead.' 'We're not bound that way!' "

It was still an era of "home remedies" for the seaman caught in thick fog. If visual signals (lighthouses, beacons, makeshift buoys, and the like) were of little use at those times, the navigator had to depend on his other senses. Some old salts claimed to be able to find their way along fog-shrouded coastlines with their noses, sniffing out familiar landmarks. But most agreed that sound was a more reliable guide. Cannons, as we have

seen, served for a while, though the most as-siduous cannoneer soon tired of firing off a warning shot (at considerable expense for gunpowder) every half-hour or so.

Fog bells came into use around 1820 at Maine's West Quoddy Head Lighthouse, though it was some years before bells were cast large enough to send out the required sound. Signal bells, either at lighthouses or on buoys offshore, had a lasting popularity with seamen. At Owl's Head Light, the keeper's daughter owned a springer spaniel named Spot who kept watch for passing boats and, upon seeing one, would give several sharp tugs on the bell rope, then rush to the shore to bark at the boat when it answered with either its bell or a whistle. Spot's vigilance was said to have paid off one gloomy night when his barking set the Matinicus mailboat back on course.

But foghorns became the wave of the future, on the Northeast coast as elsewhere. The early ones were simply whistles mounted on steam boilers. Firing a boiler, however, could become as onerous a job as shooting off a cannon, and there were attempts to use sea power to force compressed air through a whistle. Because the sea often remains comparatively calm in fog (wave-building winds can disperse fogbanks), its power was not dependable.

Nevertheless, the groaner, a whistle buoy, became a fixture along Maine's coast. It is essentially a cylinder, in a sleeve, that moves up and down with the motion of the waves. Air is forced out of the device with each plunge. Its sound (which some compare to that of a sick cow) varies with the wave action, coming at frequent intervals in a short, heavy chop and at a more stately pace in long, lazy swells.

The chief fog signals, however, have remained in and around lighthouses. The true foghorn appeared in the late 19th Century with the two-tone diaphone, a device in which compressed air was forced through a slotted reciprocating piston. In the 1880s diaphragm horns, which produced signals of varying pitch with a vibrating disk diaphragm, came into use. Their deep moans, familiar to anyone who has spent time at the shore (they are said to have driven more than one lightkeeper mad!), came to supplement and often replace the siren fog signals developed in the United States as early as 1868. Even these machines were recognized quite early on as far from foolproof, since no signal acts in a vacuum.

"While aerial fog signals furnish a very valuable aid to navigation under weather conditions when assistance is most needed, yet they are subject to a number of aberrations so that they cannot be implicitly relied upon," wrote George R. Putnam in his 1917 book *Lighthouses and Lightships of the United States.* "A signal is sometimes lost at much less than its normal range, and not infrequently a signal may be lost and at a greater distance again heard distinctly. These phenomena are associated with the refraction and reflection of sound waves.

"Sound travels faster with the wind than against it; while the direct effect is small, as the velocity of the wind is but a small percentage of that of sound, the differential effect may be important, as the velocity of the wind ordinarily increases considerably with altitude above the Earth. In such case the sound waves moving against the wind will be deflected up, over the head of the observer, and moving with the wind will be deflected down, towards the Earth. If the surface and higher winds are in different or opposite directions, the effects become more complex. Sound also travels faster in a heated atmosphere than in a cooler one, and therefore when the strata of air near the Earth's surface are more heated than those above, there will be a tendency to tilt the sound waves upward."

The introduction of electricity often reduced work, and new technology has increased the volume of the signals. Many lighthouses, with foghorns as well as lights, are fully automated; mechanisms that are extremely sensitive respond to increased moisture in the air at some distance and turn on the equipment. Maine fishermen, who often used to keep their boats in the harbor during a fog, now venture offshore with the aid of sophisticated onboard electronic equipment, including loran and radar, that not only tells them exactly where they are but what obstacles lie in their path.

Yet I still think back on scenes of the recent past, with a fogbank as the backdrop. Late at night, when the mists closed in quickly, a number of hardy souls were out on the mudflats at low tide, digging marine worms for the sport-fishing market. Suddenly the little cove where they parked their old cars came alive in a glow of headlights and a blaring of auto horns: One of their colleagues had not returned. Almost simultaneously, lights went on in the windows of shoreline camps where summer visitors were trying to sleep, and there came angry cries of "Quiet!" But the wormers in the cove kept honking horns and blinking lights until their tardy friend, guided by the uproar, came trudging out of the fog, only minutes ahead of the incoming tide, his buckets filled with a pink and pulpy mess of bloodworms.

And then there was Purcell Corbett, a lobsterman in Cutler, Maine, who found a comfortable sideline in transporting birdwatchers to the puffin colony on Machias Seal Island, nine miles off the coast. No fancy equipment for Captain Corbett, just a compass and an old hand-held horn that reminded passengers more of a New Year's tooter than a device that could mean the difference between an uneventful voyage and disaster.

Fog was no deterrent. Purcell Corbett simply looked at his compass and headed out of Cutler Harbor in his big lobster boat. When he judged he was in the vicinity of the island, he stopped periodically, turned off his engine, lifted the battered old metal horn to his lips, and gave a long, deep bellow. Then, because the island is the site of a Canadian lighthouse and Canadian boats fish in its vicinity, he listened intently for a reply. If he detected the sound of an answering blast he gave a toot or two of his own, turned on his engine again, and proceeded with caution. If there was no reply he went on for a few more minutes and repeated the process. Like all his passengers, we had implicit confidence in his ability to get us to Machias Seal Island and back.

One foggy day, a Canadian fishing boat appeared out of the fog, just off Corbett's bow. A crash occurred seconds later, and our friend did not come out of the succeeding Coast Guard inquiry in the best possible light. Purcell Corbett was no longer the operator of a public conveyance.

For what follows, it is well to keep in mind how very little water is needed to create a true fog. A U.S. Coast Guard bulletin that was published in 1916 reported on the results of studies made on a research voyage through thick fog on the Grand Banks of Newfoundland.

"Assume that one cannot see beyond one hundred feet," the scientists wrote. "A block of fog three feet wide, six feet high, and one hundred feet long contains less than one-seventh of a glass of liquid water. This water is distributed among 60 billion drops."

Small potatoes, perhaps, but often it is enough to sustain life in regions where one would not think it possible.

True deserts are among the most hostile places on Earth for living things. Rain is scarce, and fogs are usually even scarcer because warm air can hold more moisture than cold air. Exceptions include deserts along the Pacific coasts of Baja California and Chile, and the Namib, on the southwestern coast of Africa. All are long and narrow and adjacent to inshore cold-water upwelling. M.K. Seely, a biologist working in the Namib, discovered that several species of beetles have managed to make a living for themselves in the long intervals between rains. Remarkably, none of these beetles has yet evolved any anatomical adaptations to make use of fog water.

Rather, these desert dune beetles developed behavioral patterns for drinking the water deposited during irregular visitations of fog. Several kinds of beetles drink fog-water droplets that condense on vegetation or stones. Another beetle, round and short-legged, digs a trench and drinks the water that condenses on the ridges of sand that border it. Meanwhile, a long-legged species uses a technique called "fog basking," with its hard, shiny dorsum, or back, serving as a condensation surface.

"By assuming a head-down stance on or near the dune crest and orienting the linear axis of the body towards the fog-bearing wind [it] can collect fog water," Seely wrote in the publication *Oecologia*. "The water droplets coalesce and glide down to the mouth, where they are consumed."

But fog, like wind and rain, seems to be off-putting to other insects. Jeremy A. Rudd, in a 1986 article in the British journal *Nature in Cambridgeshire*, described a survey he made of the kinds and numbers of mosquitoes visiting Wicken Fen. Apparently not satisfied with the printed forms left in the fen for victims to fill out, he put himself in hazard.

Offering his blood to foraging mosquitoes on several occasions, Rudd usually did a brisk business. During one reporting period, however, fog settled in, and there was no sign of mosquitoes. I have considered a similar experiment on the foggy coast of Maine, but the passion for pure science sputters only faintly in my own breast.

Although the crafters of thrillers usually leave us with the impression that fog is the enemy of virtue, cloaking only the most mischievous affairs, history shows that heroes, too, have sometimes made good use of dense cover. It is said that General George Washington escaped complete disaster and a sudden end to the colonists' hopes by spiriting his surviving forces out of the British army's clutches under cover of fog after the battle of

Beachcombers and gulls, Old Orchard Beach, Maine (Stephen O. Muskie photo).

Long Island in 1776. Napoleon also lived to fight another day when he eluded a British fleet in fog and returned to France from Egypt in 1799.

But it must be admitted that fog is more likely to upset than abet human plans. Here a comparison with birds may be instructive. Birds, especially during the early stages of their migration, tend to land if they fly into thick fog. Those that continue often come to grief, and there are reports of various species, notably ducks, crashing into buildings, trees, and wires. Arthur Cleveland Bent, in his *Life Histories of North American Gallinaceous Birds,* quoted an observer of one of the many catastrophes to which the passenger pigeon was polarized in the late 19th Century, this time in Michigan:

"On one occasion an immense flock of young birds became bewildered in a fog while crossing Crooked Lake and, descending, struck the water and perished by thousands. The shore for miles was covered a foot or more deep with them. The old birds rose above the fog and none were killed."

Fog is said to kill and injure more humans (indirectly) than does any other meteorological hazard. A sampling of recent newspaper clippings suggests the harm to people and property:

√ Scattered fog caused a 118-car chain-reaction accident on a major West German autobahn that injured nineteen people, five of them critically.

√ A freighter carrying 23,000 tons of ore sank after colliding with a car-carrier ship in dense fog about fifteen miles off the coast of California, near Santa Barbara. The accident prompted dire warnings from environmentalists, who said that the freighter's spilled cargo—a mixture of copper, iron, and sulfur concentrates—could cause serious pollution.

√ When thousands of passengers stampeded onto a fog-shrouded ferry in Shanghai, China, eleven were killed and seventy-six injured.

√ A speeding bus plowed into mourners in a funeral procession at a village 450 miles south of Cairo, Egypt. Thirteen people were killed and nine injured in the accident, which occurred in a heavy fog.

√ Grieving relatives pressed on through mud and mist to climb to the burned wreckage of a Boeing 727 jet that had crashed in a steep mountain rainforest in Colombia, killing all 140 aboard. Officials said fog had reduced visibility near the mountain.

Now we know that fog's impact on humans goes beyond its capacity for blinding us to other hazards. It can be a hazard itself, for it carries deadly freight. In that manifestation it has a special name—"smog," a portmanteau word combining "smoke" and "fog" that dates back to 1905. A product of the industrial revolution, smog arises from the burning of fossil fuels, when nitrogen oxides react with hydrocarbons and sunlight. Thick and persistent, it often lies over a city, trapped beneath a layer of warm air.

Smog gained its reputation over Los Angeles, where Hollywood comedians made it the butt of jokes. It has, however, been abuilding over cities for generations, causing irritation and illness, especially among children, the elderly, and people with chronic lung problems. At Donora, Pennsylvania, in 1948, twenty persons died during a persistent smog, and five thousand became ill.

London's "pea soup," a compound of water vapor and various particles and pollutants, was for a time the granddaddy of all smog fogs. T.S. Eliot evoked it in a famous passage from his early poem "The Love Song of J. Alfred Prufrock":

The yellow fog that rubs its back
*   upon the window-panes,*
The yellow smoke that rubs its muzzle
*   on the window-panes,*
Licked its tongue into the corners of
*   the evening,*
Lingered upon the pools that stand
*   in drains,*
Let fall upon its back the soot that
*   falls from chimneys,*
Slipped by the terrace, made a sudden
*   leap,*
And seeing that it was a soft October
*   night,*
Curled once about the house, and
*   fell asleep.*

Finally, in 1952, all the elements combined to create a killer smog over London. More than 4,000 people died. Strangely, no one realized, even when the smog was thickest, that it was anything out of the ordinary. The appalling truth emerged only when the authorities, reviewing isolated figures supplied by various hospitals, saw that there had been an enormous upsurge in the number of deaths of patients who had pulmonary diseases. Among those who became desperately ill was T.S. Eliot, who suffered from lung problems for much of his life.

This disaster caused the British authorities to take strong action. Clean air legislation, passed in 1956, cut pollution dramatically at its source and gave Londoners the prolonged periods of sunlight they had not enjoyed since the 18th Century.

That success story offers no grounds for complacency. Fog, more and more, is giving back to us exactly what we pour into the atmosphere. Studies in California's Central Valley, where the fog sits for long periods, reveal that it holds residues of more than a dozen agricultural chemicals, mainly organophosphates. Blown into the air with dust after application and eventually mingled with fog, the chemicals are often carried to distant areas. In the Central Valley, they tend to be left with the condensed moisture on vegetation, fruits, and vegetables. No one really knows what this phenomenon portends for human health.

Further bad news comes from researchers who have proved the long-held supposition that fog actually speeds up the concentration of pollution in the atmosphere. Brigham Young University scientists, for instance, discovered that clouds (including fog) convert sulfur dioxide to sulfuric acid at about *ten times* the rate that occurs in cloudless weather. Acid fog is as much a part of modern life—and vegetative death—as acid rain.

It would not be quite true to say that everybody talks about the fog but no one does anything about it. There have been attempts, locally and periodically, to disperse the stuff when enough people thought the problems it caused were acute. Application of heat has been tried, at considerable expense. George H.T. Kimble, in his 1955 book, *Our American Weather,* described one such "fire treatment":

"During World War II, when round-the-clock aircraft patrols were frequently necessary, many a British runway was kept open in thick weather with the help of gasoline. The device employed was simple. It consisted of using a series of perforated pipes, laid along the edges of a runway, through which gasoline vapor could be sprayed and then set afire. The intense heat generated by the resulting flames evaporated the excess moisture in the air and so 'burned off' the fog. The cost, however, was considerable. Fifteen million gallons of gasoline was consumed over a period of two and one-half years in bringing in 2,500 fogbound planes. Needless to say, few commercial airlines could afford to expend 6,000 gallons of gasoline per plane per landing."

Dry ice, which does not melt but turns directly into a gas, is cheaper. So are silver iodide and some other nucleating agents, and they have been used sporadically to disperse fogs and keep airports open. But the record suggests that man is better at poisoning fog than in clearing it from trouble spots.

Powerful stuff, fog. The stuff of life and

Fishermen's homes on Grand Manan gilded in gray (Stephen Homer).

death; of dreams and melodrama, great pictures and poetry. Shakespeare, the archpoet who transformed our language and sometimes prefigured our history, drenched *Macbeth* in fog. In the play's very opening, the three witches chant:

Fair is foul, and foul is fair:
Hover through the fog and filthy air.

England later seemed to fill up with "the fog and filthy air," toward which the British came to have a proprietary feeling, especially when it descended on their capital. There it was called, in the spirit of Cockney humor, "a London particular," emphasizing its uniqueness among others of its kind. In Dickens' *Bleak House,* Esther Summerson arrived in London and found the streets so full of dense, brown smoke that she asked if there was a great fire somewhere.

"O dear no, miss," she was told. "This is a London particular... A fog, miss."

Dickens, appropriately, fixed that kind of fog in the minds of readers everywhere, and in *Bleak House* it saturates all strands of the narrative. Here, right at the beginning, he constructs in classic Dickensian prose the medium in which his characters will play out their various destinies:

"Fog everywhere. Fog up the river, where it flows among green aits and meadows; fog down the river, where it rolls defiled among the tiers of shipping, and the waterside pollutions of a great (and dirty) city. Fog on the Essex marshes, fog on the Kentish heights. Fog creeping into the cabooses of collier-brigs; fog lying out on the yards, and hov-

ering in the rigging of great ships; fog droop-
ing on the gunwales of barges and small
boats. Fog in the eyes and throats of ancient
Greenwich pensioners, wheezing by the fire-
sides of their wards; fog in the stem and bowl
of the afternoon pipe of the wrathful skipper, down in his close cabin; fog cruelly
pinching the toes and fingers of his shivering
little 'prentice boy on deck. Chance people
on the bridges peeping over the parapets into
a nether sky of fog, with fog all round them,
as if they were up in a balloon, and hanging
in the misty clouds.

"Gas looming through the fog in divers
places in the streets, much as the sun may,
from the spongy fields, be seen to loom by
husbandman and ploughboy. Most of the
shops lighted two hours before their time—
as the gas seems to know, for it has a haggard
and unwilling look.

"The raw afternoon is rawest, and the
dense fog is densest, and the muddy streets
are muddiest, near the leaden-headed old
obstruction, appropriate ornament for the
threshold of a leaden-headed old corporation: Temple Bar. And hard by Temple
Bar, in Lincoln's Inn Hall, at the very heart of
the fog, sits the Lord High Chancellor in his
High Court of Chancery.

"Never can there come fog too thick,
never can there come mud and mire too
deep, to assort with the groping and floun-
dering condition which this High Court of
Chancery, most pestilent of hoary sinners,
holds, this day, in the sight of heaven and
earth."

Dickens' novel is heavy with the "fog-
giness" of the arcane legalities that blight
people's lives in Chancery and the madness
that overwhelms the men and women victim-
ized by it. The murk mingles with soot and
smoke and grease and a kind of smoldering
fire that ultimately flares up in the breast of
the grotesque Krook and, in reducing him to
cinders, adds their unspeakable filth to the
enveloping fog.

Joseph Conrad saw London through a seaman's eyes, tinctured with romance but also
with a kind of brooding grandeur that built
an enduring nimbus over this, "the biggest,
and the greatest town on Earth." Marlow, the
yarn-spinner of *Heart of Darkness,* looks
back upriver on the city from the deck of the
"cruising yawl" *Nellie:*

"And farther west on the upper reaches
the place of the monstrous town was still
marked ominously on the sky, a brooding
gloom in sunshine, a lurid glare under the
stars."

Visiting painters, of course, took the London atmosphere to their imaginative hearts.

*Morning fog over a farm near Ottawa, Illinois
(Richard Hamilton Smith photo).*

Great black backed gulls on pilings of an abandoned wharf, Yarmouth (Stephen Homer).

If the natives looked on the fog in an upbeat fashion, speaking of the dawning of another "silver day," Whistler saw the city as "Nocturnes," bathed in blue, gray, and gold. Claude Monet fastened on those great, solid buildings planted amid the vapor and remarked that the city's "regular, massive blocks become grandiose in that mysterious cloak." The art historian Malcolm Warner, who selected the paintings for a 1987 exhibition on the various images of London captured by visiting painters, thought that fog was the most graphic feature of the city they had brought out.

"In the 18th Century, the fog was a nuisance to anyone trying to understand London as the modern Rome because it conjured up all the wrong associations," Warner wrote in the exhibition's catalog. "But as London came to seem a depressing, threatening experience, the fog, enhanced in reality by increasing pollution, began to loom larger in the imagination, suggesting both [the city's] grimness and its vast incomprehensibility, seeming to sum up the whole place."

Fog, as a manifestation of a certain kind of light, has been important to painters and absolutely vital to writers and moviemakers who deal in thrills or horror. Sir Arthur Conan Doyle, one of the founders of the modern arm of the trade, could take a villainous character and a wisp of fog, throw in a bloodcurdling shriek, and whip up a deliciously poisonous stew. After nearly ninety years, *The Hound of the Baskervilles* remains steeped in terror:

"Over the great Grimpen Mire there hung a dense, white fog. It was drifting slowly in our direction and banked itself up like a wall on that side of us, low but thick and well defined. The moon shone on it, and it looked like a great shimmering ice-field, with the heads of the distant tors as rocks borne upon its surface. Holmes's face was turned towards it, and he muttered impatiently as he watched its sluggish drift."

With good reason did the incomparable detective mutter in vexation and, a moment later, cry out in alarm. Never was a fog so sinister and murderous! In it lurked that "hound of hell" that threatened to upset all of Holmes's well-laid plans, and bring doom to still another Baskerville. But it was a benignant fog, too—confounding at last the wretch Stapleton and sending him to his just deserts in the dreadful ooze of the Grimpen Mire.

And so at night the Earth often works its alchemy. The darkening sky closes in, the land and water seem to exhale their vaporous breath, and a foghorn sounds through the deepening gloom. Then scientists give way to poets and dreamers.

IV

THE NATURALISTS

JIM CORBETT: THE RELUCTANT EXECUTIONER

TEXT BY GEOFFREY C. WARD

The tiger lay on its back behind a log, paws in the air, fast asleep. The hunter crept closer, rifle raised, until he was within five feet, then fired two bullets into the animal's brain. The tiger died without moving. It had been steadily killing and eating human beings for years, one every few days. The last—a woman cutting grass in the forest—had been killed less than a week before the hunter tracked him down. This was the climax of an arduous pursuit that had gone on for several weeks up and down the steep slopes of the Himalayan foothills in the full blast of an Indian May. At the sound of the shots, a crowd of villagers hurried to the site to see for themselves that the animal that had terrorized them for so long was truly dead and to cheer the man who had risked his own life to rid them of it.

The successful hunter, a tall, slim, middle-aged Briton named Jim Corbett, might have been forgiven had he shared at least a little of their exultation. Instead, he felt depressed. "The finish," he wrote later, "had not been
satisfactory, for I had killed the animal . . . in his sleep." He continued: "My personal feelings in the matter are I know of little interest to others, but it occurs to me that possibly you also might think it was not cricket, and in that case I should like to put some arguments before you that I used on myself, in the hope that you will find them more satisfactory than I did. These arguments were (a) the tiger was a man-eater that was better dead than alive, (b) therefore it made no difference whether he was awake or asleep when killed, and (c) that had I walked away when I saw his belly moving up and down [indicating that he was sleeping] I should have been morally responsible for the deaths of all the human beings he killed thereafter. All good and sound arguments, you will admit, for having acted as I did; but the regret remains that through fear of the consequences to myself or for fear of losing the only chance I might ever get, or possibly a combination of the two, I did not awaken the sleeping animal and give him a sporting chance."*

A bust of Jim Corbett at the entrance to Corbett National Park.

112

"The Tiger," Jim Corbett wrote in *Man-eaters of Kumaon,* his first and best-loved book, "is a large-hearted gentleman with boundless courage." Such courtly anthropomorphism is understandably out of fashion these days, but the same description could justly be applied to the man who wrote it. For Corbett represented within himself—as hunter and conservationist, author and outdoorsman, and loyal subject of the Crown—all the gentlemanly attributes of the British imperial system at its best. The tragedy was that, partly because he also shared that system's worst delusions, he became its victim, ending his days in sad, self-imposed exile from the land he never stopped loving.

Edward James Corbett was born in India and therefore a "Domiciled Englishman"—the scornful epithet was "country-bottled"—relegated to the lowest rank among India's white rulers, whose caste system was only slightly more yielding than that of those they ruled. Domiciled Englishmen were thought better than coolies by upper-class Britons—they were welcome, for example, on the Upper Mall in the Himalayan hill station of Naini Tal, where Corbett was born in 1875, from which Indians and beasts of burden were expressly barred—and they were thought more desirable than persons of mixed British and Indian ancestry. But they could never expect to serve in prestigious administrative posts or to climb very high in the army, even though without them and their forebears there would have been no British Raj at all.

Corbett's own father, Christopher Corbett, the Naini Tal postmaster, had helped lift the siege of Delhi during the 1857 mutiny. That sudden and bloody rebellion by Indian troops thought faithful to the British Queen had traumatized the Raj. Afterwards, the British never fully trusted their Indian subjects. Corbett and his brothers and sisters were steeped in mutiny lore: Their father's younger brother had been tied to a tree and burned alive by the rebels; their mother's father had been pulled from his horse and hacked to death. No matter how gentle and amiable Indians seemed, the children were taught, one had always to be on guard.

Christopher Corbett died suddenly when James was four, leaving his wife with a summer home above Naini Tal, a winter home fifteen miles down the mountain road at Kaladhungi, and a turbulent brood of twelve children to raise and educate on a widow's meager pension. The Corbetts were poor but proud. Appearances were kept up. Stoicism and self-sacrifice were encouraged. His mother, Corbett recalled, "though she had

G. ALLAN BROWN

the courage of Joan of Arc and Nurse Clavell combined, was as gentle and timid as a dove."

He remembered his boyhood as a sort of forest idyll. Lying in bed at Kaladhungi, he listened night after night to the cries of the animals that filled the dark surrounding forests, learning first to understand and eventually to mimic nearly all of them. (As a grown man he could call a serpent eagle down out of the sky using a split reed to imitate the piercing call of a fawn in distress, and he once impersonated a leopard so persuasively that a British hunter and a leopard crept toward him simultaneously.) In the early mornings the small boy eagerly paced the sandy bed of the Baur River that ran near the house, studying fresh tracks to discover what had happened there the night before. Corbett's uncanny understanding of the plants and animals and birds of the Kumaon Hills had virtually been bred into him.

Corbett's earliest shooting was done to fill the family larder. He had to account for every shell. "Good shooting," the same friend wrote, "was to him an obligation rather than an accomplishment." But his increasingly frequent trips into the forest may have had another meaning, too. The Corbett household must have been a tumultuous place: Years later, Corbett would confess that, as adults, neither he nor his older sister, Maggie, ever felt "happy in a crowd." By the age of nine, Corbett was spending several days at a time in the forest. An aged family gardener sometimes accompanied him, but he slept in

In a rare picture, Jim Corbett poses with the Bachelor of Powalgarh, a tiger of "magnificent proportions"—measuring 10 feet 7 inches from nose to tip of tail. The kill occurred in 1930.

the open, and his only real protection was an ancient muzzle-loading shotgun whose one good barrel was lashed to the stock with brass wire.

He attended school at Naini Tal, finding time between classes to shoot and prepare the skins of some 480 species of hill birds for a cousin who was preparing a field guide. Then, at seventeen, he signed on with the Indian railways, one of the few organizations hospitable to young Domiciled Englishmen. He was a fuel inspector at first, supervising the felling of timber, and then he became a transshipment inspector at Mokameh Ghat, a dusty outstation on the bank of the Ganges east of Benares. There was nothing remotely glamorous about his job, which for just over two decades consisted of seeing to it that a million tons of goods were ferried across the river from one rail line to another every year. But he did gain an extraordinary reputation for industry and fairness among the Indian

laborers who worked for him, eating nothing but lentils and unleavened bread when times were lean, just as they did, and distributing eighty percent of his own annual profits among the men at Christmastime.

Nor was there anything especially adventurous about his daily life after he left the railway at thirty-nine, without ever having moved up in its hierarchy. He moved back to Naini Tal, went into the hardware and real-estate business, and did about as well as a country-born Englishman could expect. He served on the town council and presented the town with a brightly painted band shell. He was not, until very late in life, asked to join the Naini Tal Yacht Club. Even after he did join, a friend recalled, he rarely went there, being unused to "the elevated society." Winters were spent at Kaladhungi in a small bungalow at the edge of a village called Choti Haldwani, of which he and his sister Maggie became the benevolent proprietors. Corbett

114

adjudicated family disputes among his tenants, calmed tension between Hindus and Muslims, provided improved seed; he even acted as unofficial physician, dispensing pills and unguents to sick or injured villagers. And he acted as their protector, too, building a three-mile stone wall around the village and its fields to keep deer and wild boar out of their crops and eliminating any predators that menaced their cattle and buffalo.

His India was always that of the peasant. "Simple, honest, brave, loyal, hard-working souls," he called them once, "whose daily prayer to God, and to whatever Government is in power, is to give them security of life and of property to enable them to enjoy the fruits of their labors." Modern India—urban, educated, interested in politics, and impatient with British rule—was alien to him, and always menacing.

Corbett never married, and when an intrusive interviewer once asked him why, he responded with uncharacteristic vehemence. "It has been my privilege," he said, "no, I have had the *honor,* to make a home for the best mother and sister in the world." Corbett's mother died in 1924, but Maggie remained with him until the end of his life, listening to his jungle stories and brewing the endless pots of strong tea that seem to have been the closest Jim Corbett ever came to vice.

There were thousands of other Britons scattered in small places all across India in those days, living similarly quiet lives, largely unknown beyond the villages over which they held sway. It was Corbett's shooting skill and encyclopedic knowledge of the jungle that set him apart. As early as 1906, requests began to reach him begging that he come up into the hills to track down a tiger or leopard that had begun to prey on man. Sometimes the afflicted villagers themselves petitioned him, their genuine terror evident beneath the inflated language of the scribes whose pens they hired:

Respected Sir,
We the public are in great distress. By the fear of the tiger we cannot watch our wheat crop so the deers have nearly ruined it. We cannot go into the forest for the fodder grass nor can we enter our cattles into the forest to graze . . . We have heard that your kind self have killed many man-eater tigers and leopards. So we the public venture to suggest that you very kindly take trouble to come to this place and shoot this tiger and save the public from this calamity. For this act of kindness the public will be highly obliged and will pray for your long life and prosperity.

GUNTER ZIESLER

More often, local British officials did the asking, having exhausted every other remedy. But it took considerable evidence to coax Corbett into the field. He believed that any animal which had struck once or twice under special circumstances—while guarding cubs, for example, or when disturbed on a fresh kill—should be given the benefit of the doubt. It was only habitual man-eaters that interested him, and even when there was no question that an animal was guilty, he never volunteered to shoot it; as a Domiciled Englishman he would not go where he was not wanted. And he always set two conditions: All offers of a reward had to be withdrawn before he arrived, and all other hunters had to leave the forest. His reasons were at once principled and practical. "I am sure all sportsmen share my aversion to being classed as a reward-hunter," he wrote, "and are as anxious as I am to avoid being shot."

Corbett consented to hunt down a dozen man-eaters between 1906 and 1941. There is no way of estimating how many human lives his efforts saved, but the combined total of men, women, and children those twelve animals killed before he stopped them was more than 1,500. (Corbett's very first man-eater, the Champawat tiger, alone was responsible for 436 deaths.)

The man-eating leopard of Rudraprayag, the most celebrated of all Corbett's quarries and the only one to which he devoted an entire book, officially killed 150 people between 1918 and 1926. But because it operated along the twisting mountain trail that leads up to the Hindu shrines of Kedernath and Badrinath, to which some 60,000 pilgrims made their way on foot each year, its depredations were widely publicized, both in

The Corbett house at Kaladhungi.

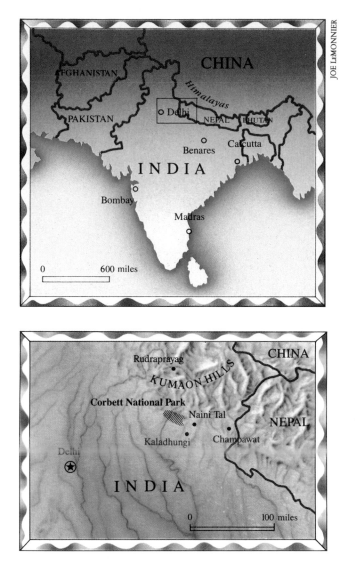

Finally, A. W. Ibbotson, deputy commissioner of the district and an old hunting companion of Corbett's, persuaded him to try his hand. Corbett had been reluctant to intrude at first: "I imagined that people were falling over each other in their eagerness...and that in those circumstances a stranger would not be welcome." In any case, he arrived in the early autumn of 1925.

Once Corbett was on the man-eater's trail, however, his tenacity was astonishing. One of the reasons his accounts of his own adventures are so vivid and persuasive is that he never flinched from detailing his own weakness and frustration. *The Man-Eating Leopard of Rudraprayag* is a chronicle of terror as well as bravery, of missed opportunities as well as jungle skills, of bad luck as well as persistence. Corbett sat over the corpse of a pregnant woman in the rain most of one night, and in the pitch blackness failed to make out the leopard as it slipped beneath him, its passage marked only by an eery, inexplicable sound, he said, "like the soft rustle of a woman's silk dress."

He spent twenty nights alone on the top of a sixty-foot tower overlooking the only bridge across a gorge, tormented by stinging ants and clinging to the tower's flat, featureless top to keep from being blown off by the stiff winds that whipped up the valley. He was rewarded for all his time and trouble by the sight of precisely one animal trotting over the bridge, an oblivious jackal.

Sleeping in a thorn enclosure, he woke to the screams of his cook, who had opened one eye to see the leopard crouched above him in a tree, ready to spring. Before Corbett could get his rifle to his shoulder, the animal bounded away. A few nights later, he was sure he'd caught the man-eater in a leg trap; he fired at the struggling animal in the darkness and succeeded only in snapping the chain that held it there. Corbett tracked it down on foot and killed it—only to find that, although it had earlier stalked a human victim, it was the wrong leopard. After ten weeks of this, Corbett was near collapse from exhaustion. Ibbotson ordered him home to recuperate.

It took him nearly three months, during which the leopard killed ten more people. He tried to trap it again when he got back the following spring; and once the trap did close on the man-eater's leg, but two of its steel teeth had broken off, allowing the animal just room enough to slip out again. Corbett spent another night in a tree so fiercely lashed by the wind that he had to tie his rifle to the trunk and tear off as many branches as he could reach to cut down wind resistance.

India and abroad. For eight years, no one dared move along that road after dusk; no villager living in the nearby hills stirred from his home.

The leopard was a big male, strong enough to carry his kills up to four miles if necessary, and it had grown very bold, first taking only victims foolish enough to sleep outdoors, then banging down doors or leaping through windows to get at them, finally methodically clawing its way through the mud walls of their huts. Rewards were posted. Hundreds of special gun licenses were issued. Amateur sportsmen and local officials sat up for the leopard. Army officers were encouraged to spend their leaves tracking it. Nothing worked. The animal eluded every trap. Poisons seemed only to encourage it. Twenty other leopards were destroyed, but the man-eater remained at large and hungry, and angry questions began to be asked in the British Parliament.

Nonetheless, he managed to call up the leopard and lure it toward him; all seemed to be progressing well, finally. Then the man-eater encountered a female leopard en route and settled down to an evening of noisy mating out of rifle range.

Still another night was spent sitting on the ground in a village courtyard only a few yards from the half-eaten body of a small boy. There was no moon, and when Corbett suddenly felt fur rub against his bare knee he was sure that the leopard had found him at last. Instead, it was a small kitten that had been locked out of its hut. He placed it inside his jacket, where it purred and fell asleep. The leopard did approach the village but again encountered another leopard, a male this time, setting off a long yowling fight during which the kill was forgotten.

Finally, on the last of eleven nights spent in a big mango tree on the pilgrim road, the man-eater appeared in plain sight. A flashlight was attached to Corbett's rifle. He clicked it on, took aim, and fired. At the shot, the flashlight blinked out. But the leopard at last lay dead.

Characteristically, Corbett's initial emotion was regret. The dead leopard's "only crime, not against the laws of nature but against the laws of man," he wrote, "was that he had shed human blood with no object of terrorizing man, but only in order that he might live." His friend Ibbotson literally danced with joy at the news. Corbett asked for a pot of tea, took a hot bath, and went to sleep. Later in the day, thousands of people from the surrounding hills converged to see the leopard and offer thanks to their deliverer. Corbett was persuaded to receive them, standing tall and silent as, one by one, they filed past to pour rose and marigold petals around his feet.

Like that other solitary British hero, Lawrence of Arabia, Corbett seems always to have been dissatisfied even with his most dramatic triumphs, to have genuinely feared and distrusted the praise his actions won. Like Lawrence, too, he appears to have relished punishing himself. "No greater pleasure can a man know than the sudden cessation of great pain," Corbett once quoted approvingly. He had no bedroom of his own at Kaladhungi for many years, sleeping in a tent beside the house while his sister slept inside. Once on a tiger's trail, he often marched through the hills at a twenty-five-mile-a-day clip, eating nothing for up to sixty-four hours at a stretch. Such strenuous deprivation "had no injurious effect upon me," he wrote, "beyond taking a little flesh off my bones."

In 1929 a heavy rifle went off accidentally beside his left ear. The eardrum was pierced, the inner ear scorched. Nonetheless, when Corbett was asked to hunt down the Talla Des man-eater, a tigress responsible for another 150 deaths, he did not hesitate. The pursuit lasted several weeks, during which an abcess steadily grew within his ear, closing his left eye, immobilizing his head and neck, making every step agony. He never even slowed his pace, sitting up night after night though half-blind and almost wholly deaf (his right ear had been damaged earlier), and nearly incoherent with pain and fever. Finally, as he waited for the man-eater in the branches of still another tree, the abcess burst. "Not into my brain as I feared it would," he reported cheerily, "but out through my nose and left ear." He fainted, but he got his tigress.

News of his exploits inevitably reached the newspapers and was passed around the best clubs. The rich and well-born began to seek him out. He was asked to orchestrate elaborate shoots for important people: generals, government officials, maharajahs, the viceroy himself, Lord Linlithgow. These hunts were the antithesis of his own stealthy pursuits. Hundreds of beaters shouted their way through the forests and grasslands, and specially trained elephants delicately retrieved with their trunks the partridge and peafowl the guests and their ladies downed. Corbett professed to be astonished at all the attention he received—"I, a mere man in the street, with no official connection to Government." But, in fact, he had become the most famous sportsman in India. It cannot have been lost on him that when he was in his forest even the most socially exalted amateur had to stand in his shadow.

By the mid-1930s, Corbett had himself almost entirely abandoned hunting. A clergyman who knew him slightly claimed that his conversion came after having been sickened during a duck shoot in which three hundred birds were killed, but no such epiphany may have been necessary. It was the solitude of the jungle and what Corbett called his "knowledge of the language and habits of the jungle folk" that had always drawn him, not the shooting. In his later years he rarely fired at anything larger than the jungle fowl that scratched along the paths near Kaladhungi; when villagers appealed to him to shoot the occasional tiger or leopard that had taken one of their stray animals, he now refused, paying compensation instead out of his own pocket.

He became fascinated with the challenge of filming tigers in the wild. A friend re-

An Indian leopard feeds at night on a natural kill of a nilgai antelope. Now twice the size of the original park, Corbett contains a large share of the tiger and leopard populations of India. (Gertrud and Helmut Denzau)

called chancing upon Corbett as he stumbled out of a thicket not far from his summer home: "He explained that he had been trying to get a picture of a tigress, but she was in bad temper and as often as he went into the thicket she drove him out. He added, however, as one who was ready to make due allowances, that she had her cubs with her." He rarely bothered to carry a rifle during these encounters, hoping instead that he might distract an angry tiger by tossing at it the small khaki pillow on which he sat. When the whir of his camera scared off his subjects he dammed a stream not far from his home so that its gurgle would disguise the camera's grinding, then sat day after day for four months in a nearby tree until he was finally able to film seven tigers there at once.

During the 1930s, too, Corbett began to speak out publicly in defense of Indian wildlife. "A country's fauna is a sacred trust," he wrote in 1931, "and I appeal to you not to betray your trust." He served on state wildlife boards, helped found a natural-history magazine, and worked to establish India's first national park in the Kumaon Hills, a park that teemed with wildlife and was named after an old hunting patron, Lord Hailey, the governor of the United Provinces. He especially enjoyed appearing before groups of schoolchildren at Naini Tal, performing a sort of one-man jungle oratorio, during which he imitated in turn the cries of each bird and animal in the forest as it heralded the approach of a tiger. For the finale he asked that the lights be turned off in the auditorium, warned those with faint hearts to leave the room, then gave the full roar of a tiger, a sound guaranteed to electrify the most blasé schoolboy.

Corbett was sixty-four years old when World War II began, far too old for active service. But he volunteered to recruit an Indian labor corps and later to train British officers in the techniques of jungle survival they would need if they were to win Burma back from the Japanese. The strain finally told: Corbett was ravaged by tick typhus and malaria and by pneumonia that permanently affected his lungs. His weight fell from 175 to 108 pounds, and for a time it seemed unlikely that he would ever walk again, let alone reenter his beloved forests. He spent two years out of action, and perhaps in part just to fill the empty hours began to write the book that became *Man-Eaters of Kumaon*.

His idea was that profits from a modest sale of the book would benefit Indian soldiers blinded in the service of the Crown. Instead, it became an international best-seller, translated into at least twenty-seven lan-

guages, and almost universally admired by critics. (Edmund Wilson was a lonely dissenter; Corbett's style, he said, reminded him of "ruptured Kipling.")

Part of the power of Corbett's writing lies in the sometimes maddening faithfulness with which he recalls and re-creates the smallest details of his hunts. Above all, he wants his reader to know *just* how it was, no matter how long it takes to describe. The result is the kind of suspense that a professional writer, trained to be more selective, could not easily create.

In the chapter devoted to "The Chowgarh Tigers" in *Man-Eaters of Kumaon,* for example, he takes forty-odd pages to recount his two-year search for a tigress which, with her cub, had killed at least sixty-four people. Along the way he digresses to tell of encoun-

GUNTER ZIESLER

ters with mountain goats, a leopard, several tigers, and a bear and to confess that, in mistakenly shooting the cub rather than the mother while sitting up over a kill, he had inadvertently caused the deaths of an additional dozen human victims.

On the nineteenth straight day of stalking, he scrambles down a stony hillside, nearly every inch of which he describes, then lands soundlessly in a sandy streambed at the foot of a tall, sheer rock. Here he describes what happened next:

As I stepped clear of this giant slate, I looked behind me over my right shoulder and—looked straight into the tigress's face.

I would like you to have a clear picture of the situation.

The sandy bed behind the rock was quite flat. To the right of it was smooth slate fifteen feet high and leaning slightly outwards, to the left of it was a scoured-out steep bank also some fifteen feet high overhung by a dense tangle of thorn bushes, while at the far end was a slide similar to but a little higher than the one I had glissaded down. The sandy bed enclosed by these three natural walls was about twenty feet long and half as wide, and lying on it, with her forepaws stretched out and her hind legs well tucked under her, was the tigress. Her head, which was raised a few inches off her paws, was eight feet (measured later) from me, and on her face was a smile, similar to that one sees on the face of a dog welcoming his master home from a long absence.

Two thoughts flashed through my mind: one, that it was up to me to make the first

Morning mist in the Ramganga River Valley of Corbett Park.

121

move, and the other, that the move would have to be made in such a manner as not to alarm the tigress or make her nervous.

The rifle was in my right hand held diagonally across my chest [Corbett was carrying a clutch of nightjar eggs in his left, found on his way down the hill], with the safety-catch off, and in order to get it to bear on the tigress the muzzle would have to be swung round three-quarters of a circle.

The movement of swinging round the rifle, with one hand, was begun very slowly and hardly perceptibly, and when a quarter of a circle had been made, the stock came in contact with my right side. It was now necessary to extend my arm, and as the stock cleared my side, the swing was very slowly continued. My arm was now at full stretch and the weight of the rifle was beginning to tell. Only a little further now for the muzzle to go, and the tigress—who had not once taken her eyes off mine—was still looking up at me with the pleased expression still on her face.

How long it took the rifle to make the three-quarter circle, I am not in a position to say. To me, looking into the tigress's eyes and unable therefore to follow the movement of the barrel, it appeared that my arm was paralysed, and that the swing would never be completed. However, the movement was completed at last, and as soon as the rifle was pointing at the tiger's body, I pressed the trigger.

I heard the report, exaggerated in that restricted space, and felt the jar of the recoil, and but for these tangible proofs that the rifle had gone off, I might, for all the immediate result the shot produced, have been in the grip of one of those awful nightmares in which triggers are vainly pulled of rifles that refuse to be discharged at the critical moment.

For a perceptible fraction of time, the tigress remained perfectly still, and then, very slowly, her head sank on to her outstretched paws.

He had, of course, hit his quarry in the heart.

Corbett's publisher later theorized that the book's success owed a good deal to its appearance in 1944: "The end of the war was in sight. Years of massive, indiscriminate slaughter and regimentation had eroded faith in the significance of the individual. It was immensely refreshing to read of this contemporary dragon-killer, who in perfect freedom roamed the countryside cheerfully facing danger and hardship to rid the world of tigers and leopards convicted of man-eating. Sir Galahad rode again. Truth and justice had returned."

Beyond the tales of Corbett's quests, however, lies an extraordinary body of accurately observed detail about life in the Indian jungles in general and the behavior of tigers in particular. (This last, Corbett admitted, was mostly gleaned after he had given up the rifle for the camera.) Most of his independent findings have been borne out by subsequent scholars: Tigers kill with their teeth, not their paws. They do so as readily in broad daylight as they do in darkness, provided they are left undisturbed by man. A man-eater "is a tiger that has been compelled, through stress of circumstances beyond its control, to adopt a diet alien to it," and "stress is, in nine cases out of ten, wounds, and in the tenth case, old age."

A gharial lies in wait. This long-snouted crocodile has 54 upper and 48 lower teeth, ideal for grasping fish and frogs but not large prey.

He did all that he could to deflate the myth that the tiger was man's natural enemy. "The author who first used the words 'as cruel as a tiger' and 'as bloodthirsty as a tiger' when attempting to emphasize the evil character of the villain of his piece," he wrote in the opening pages of *Man-Eaters of Kumaon,* "not only showed lamentable ignorance of the animal he defamed, but coined phrases which have come into universal circulation, and which are mainly responsible for the wrong opinion of tigers held by all except the small proportion of the public who have the opportunity of forming their own opinions."

Sadly, however, the overall impact of Corbett's writing on the larger public was probably the opposite of what he intended. What we remember best from his books are the harrowing details of long nights spent sitting up over corpses; the dread of the grieving villagers huddled in their huts; the astonishing strength of even the most apparently enfeebled man-eaters, which again and again Corbett had to track down after inflicting fearful wounds. In this gory context his pleas for understanding his powerful, stealthy quarry tend to be forgotten.

Indian independence finally came in 1947. Corbett was certain it spelled disaster. The Indians were still incapable of governing themselves; that had been the central premise of the Raj and of Corbett's own beliefs. His beloved forests would now be razed or overrun; wildlife would be obliterated; Hailey Park was doomed. Finally, he was sure, once the British had gone, the Soviets would march down through his mountains to seize the subcontinent. Maggie, now seventy-two, had still more immediate fears: The Indians were sure to wreak an awful vengeance on any Britons who dared remain behind, raping and burning and killing as they had in her grandparents' time. They must flee.

The Corbetts sold their houses at Naini Tal and Kaladhungi. But where were they to go? India had been their family home for at least three generations. Corbett had only visited Britain briefly once in his life. Instead, they withdrew to the White Highlands of Kenya, where British settlers, including several of their relatives, still struggled to hold on to something of the old imperial life. They rented a cottage in the garden of the Outspan Hotel at Nyeri. It had once been occupied by that earlier model of British sportsmanship, Lord Baden-Powell, the founder of Scouting. Here the old man spent his last years, filming lions and elephants whenever he felt strong enough, feeding the twenty-six varieties of birds that fluttered in and out of the garden, and tapping out with one finger five more books—*The Man-Eating Leopard of Rudraprayag* (1948), *My India* (1952), *Jungle Lore* (1953), *The Temple Tiger and More Man-Eaters of Kumaon* (1954), and *Tree Tops* (1955)—tearing out a page and starting over whenever he made a mistake. He wrote back to India often, too, inquiring about the mustard crop at Kaladhungi, wanting reassurance that his house was being properly cared for, hinting that he might come back for a visit.

Kenya provided precious little sanctuary. The thin highlands air did not agree with Corbett. His lungs weakened steadily, but he refused even to think of moving again. "One has to live *somewhere,*" he told Maggie. The Mau Mau rebellion had begun. Maggie found a Kikuyu tribesman hidden beneath her bed one evening when her brother was away. The intruder demanded money; she refused and was knocked down as he fled.

In February 1952 Princess Elizabeth and Prince Philip visited Kenya and requested that when they spent a night at Tree Tops—a lushly appointed game-watching hut built high in the branches of an ancient ficus tree overlooking a busy waterhole—Corbett act as their guide. The twenty hours he spent there in the company of royalty was Corbett's "day of days," he wrote, more important and more filled with meaning for the old country-bottled colonial than any of the deeds for which the rest of the world remembered him. Proximity to the princess made him gush: Her face was "as fresh as a flower, no artificial aids were needed or used to enhance the bloom of her cheeks." Her approach to Tree Tops, an uneventful walk past trumpeting elephants, he pronounced one of the "most courageous acts" he had ever witnessed. He was permitted to hold her camera and pocketbook as she climbed the ladder, and later he sat between the prince and princess at dinner.

After the royal couple had gone to bed, he spent the rest of the night as he had spent so many others, in the open, sitting motionless at the top of the ladder, rifle across his lap, watching not for a tiger or a leopard this time but for terrorists. None appeared, but that same night George VI died suddenly in London, making his daughter monarch of the retreating Empire. "When I helped her into the tree she was a princess," Corbett marveled to a friend a few days later, "and when I helped her down she was a queen."

Jim Corbett died of a heart attack on April 19, 1955, and was buried in the tiny Anglican cemetery at Nyeri, 3,500 miles from his real home in India, that is, *My India.*

"In the olden days," Corbett's old friend, Lord Hailey, wrote after his death, "he would have been one of the small band of Europeans whose memory has been worshiped by Indians as that of men who were in some measure also gods." Hailey's words, like so many of Corbett's own, were tinged with affectionate condescension, but certainly in India more than most places, specifics do seem to fade with time, distinctions blur, the secular somehow becomes sanctified. A young man from Kanda, a hilltop village near which Corbett shot one of his last man-eaters, has trouble now remembering just what his grandfather had told him of the shooting. Had the tiger killed three people before Corbett came, or was it six? "Carpet-sahib was god," the aged headman of another village explained to an interviewer a few years ago. "The goddess appeared to him in person."

Corbett's old home at Kaladhungi has been transformed into a museum by the Forest Department, and its former owner's new aura of sanctity is evident everywhere among the sparse exhibits. There are not many visitors; a new road to Naini Tal has been built, and so there is no need for most travelers to pass the garden gate as they once did. Five uniformed forest officers were therefore free to accompany me through the bungalow's three small rooms one morning last spring. Around the stained walls are hung brief passages from Corbett's writings: *Any task well accomplished gives pleasure; From November to March the climate of the Himalayan foothills has no equal; The knowledge you absorb today will be added to the knowledge you will absorb tomorrow.* Unexceptional statements, but each reverently hand-lettered as if it were sacred scripture. Corbett's posthumous sainthood may owe some-

thing to the fact that he never married; Hindu sages are traditionally celibate.

I was shown several relics, including Corbett's folding steel camp bed, a big clumsy affair which I was assured had been the platform from which he shot his tigers; his crabapple walking stick, taken down from the old gun case in which it is kept for me to hold for a moment; and a cracked white cup from which he sipped his morning tea in Kenya. The officer in charge fished into a grimy, creased envelope and brought out between thumb and forefinger a single guinea fowl feather; Corbett was said to have given it to a friend a month before he died.

There have been a lot of changes since Corbett's day. For a time it seemed his darkest fears would be confirmed. There was fierce slaughter of India's wildlife, but it has slowed in recent years. Project Tiger, the international effort to preserve the species that was launched in 1973, seems to be succeeding: There are now said to be more than 4,000 tigers in India, probably more than there were when Corbett sailed away. One of the project's most important preserves has been Corbett National Park, the same Hailey Park whose survival Corbett worried over, renamed for him after his death and now nearly twice its former size.

Trucks blare past the Kaladhungi compound these days, and tractors plow the fields that Corbett's villagers worked with bullocks. But their thatch huts are still engulfed in green wheat; mangoes still ripen in the old hunter's garden; the spotted deer still steal down out of the forest to drink in the evenings. And just at sunset one day last spring, a tiger was seen sitting in the dry bed of the Baur River, not very far from where Jim Corbett saw the pug marks of his first tigers a hundred years ago.

Indian elephants at Corbett National Park.

125

Dhitu, a favorite tiger at Corbett National Park, before his killing a laborer cost him his freedom.

GUNTER ZIESLER

Located in the Himalayan foothills 180 miles northeast of Delhi, Corbett National Park, is today much as Jim Corbett himself first knew it. Blue forested hills and broad grasslands are cut by clear mountain streams and alive with birds and animals. The illusion of total wilderness is broken only by the roads that run through it, and by the hortatory slogans painted here and there in bright orange on the stony hillsides: TAKE ONLY PICTURES; LEAVE ONLY FOOTPRINTS. When, through accident or intention, its animals threaten human life nowadays, they are treated in a way that would have pleased the old sportsman.

About 11:30 in the morning of February 22, 1985, a British ornithologist named David Hunt was leading a party of eighteen birdwatchers along a dusty path in the heart of the park. Forest guard Harrak Singh walked with him, armed with an old shotgun that was loaded with buckshot and intended only to be fired into the air to discourage wild elephants from venturing too close.

Hunt had visited the park several times before and knew that no one was ever allowed to leave the paths for any reason. But, when he spotted a large and unusual owl sitting in a tree high on a slope, he and two friends decided they would climb up to see if they could get a picture. Harrak Singh's warnings were ignored.

The climb proved steep and rocky, complicated by thick tangles of lantana and bamboo. When the owl left its perch and flapped farther up the hillside, Hunt split off from his companions to try to find an easier route. His friends grew discouraged and returned to the path.

They heard a scream, then silence. Harrak Singh forced his way up the slope, shotgun in hand, until he reached the lip of a natural shelf and cautiously peered over it. The grass in front of him was smeared with bright blood. Hunt's binoculars lay nearby, their strap broken. Farther back was Hunt's

INNOCENCE

sprawled body, and beyond it, melting into the forest, was the striped form of a tiger. Harrak Singh hurried down the slope to summon help.

It took several hours for a party to assemble, and another twenty minutes or so to prod eight nervous elephants, each bearing an armed forest guard, into making their ponderous way up the steep slope. By then, the body had been carefully hidden by the tiger in a clump of bamboo.

The great cat was still nearby, some thirty yards farther up the hillside, pacing back and forth and snarling. Eight shots were fired into the air. The animal would not be scared off. Finally, the elephants were drawn up into a line between the tiger and the bamboo so that the body could be recovered. Hunt's neck had been broken; the right side of his face was crushed and the eye scooped out. His left kneecap had been removed as if by a surgeon, and a small portion of his calf appeared to have been eaten.

In the excitement, no one got a very clear description of the tiger, although one member of the party did manage to snap several blurry photographs of it.

Asok Singh, the park director, was now faced with a difficult decision. Would the killer strike again? Was this a painful but isolated incident, a tragic accident caused by human heedlessness? Or was it the beginning of a deliberate career of man-eating?

The killing had taken place within the staked-out territory of a male tiger the forest guards called Dhitu, whose disdain for visitors was legend among park personnel. He was an enormous, glossy animal, weighing perhaps 500 pounds. He was so impressive and so utterly unconcerned in the presence of humans that he had become a sort of unofficial park mascot, featured on posters and T-shirts. His huge, round pug marks were found in a riverbed not far from the hillside up which David Hunt had scrambled to his death. All the available evidence seemed to indicate that Dhitu's lifelong disdain for people had finally turned him into a killer. Reluctantly, the director announced that the celebrated tiger should be shot.

Five days later, Brijendra Singh arrived at Corbett Park. He is a short, sturdy outdoorsman, a member of the former royal family of the princely state of Kapurthala. Once a keen hunter, he has become a dedicated conservationist. He lives in a fashionable section of New Delhi but spends as much time as he can each year among Corbett Park's tigers, and takes with great seriousness his status as honorary wildlife warden. Almost exactly one year earlier, he had helped trap a tiger responsible for the death of one elephant-handler and the near-fatal mauling of another; the animal had been shipped to the Lucknow zoo, where it had subsequently died. Dhitu was a special favorite of his, and before the tiger was executed he wanted to be certain of its guilt beyond a reasonable doubt.

Brijendra Singh visited the site. The ornithologist's binoculars still lay where they had fallen from his neck at the cliff's edge. A trail of other belongings—a book of matches, Hunt's watch, several crumpled sheets of tissue—marked the trail up which he had been dragged. There was still dried blood beneath the bamboo.

That night, Brijendra Singh had a buffalo calf tied at the base of the hill. It was gone by morning, killed and hauled up the thickly grown slope. He followed the trail until he found the dead buffalo precisely where Hunt's body had been hidden. Clearly, the same tiger had hidden both kills, but there was no tiger to be seen.

The honorary wildlife warden climbed into a tree with his camera. More than three hours passed. Once he heard what sounded like the thin yowling of tiger cubs from somewhere farther up the slope. Then a striped animal appeared on the hillside above the kill. Not Dhitu, but a young tigress, her belly still loose from having recently given birth to a litter.

Brijendra Singh raised his camera and took several pictures. Later they would prove a perfect match with those taken of the animal that the shotguns of the forest guards had failed to intimidate. Her apparent fearlessness was now explained: She had been unwilling to abandon her hidden cubs.

It was now possible to reconstruct exactly what had happened on the hillside six days earlier. On that morning, the tigress had left her cubs safely secreted among the rocks higher up the slope. She had stretched out in the cool grass near the cliff's edge and there had fallen asleep. David Hunt, his eyes on the elusive owl above him, had loomed suddenly over her. Startled, frightened, she had lashed out.

Instinct had made her kill. Then it made her hide what she had killed. Finally it had made her sample that kill. But she had *only* sampled it, and there was no reason to assume she would ever repeat any part of what had now clearly been an inadvertent tragedy.

A few days after David Hunt was killed, my wife and I had a chance to see the exonerated Dhitu. We found him in a pool, up to his chin in the dark, stained water. Our elephant shook with fear as we approached, producing her own low, uneasy rumble. Though we stopped and stood less than thirty feet away from him for at least ten minutes, the tiger paid no attention to us.

After a time he hauled himself out of the water and began, as if on cue, a repertoire of tigerish activities. He rolled onto his back, lazily examined one enormous paw, and scratched his wet shoulders on the leafy forest floor. Then he stood up and, gazing intently at us for the first time, sprayed as if to mark as his own the clearing into which we had intruded, emitting a thin, astonishingly forceful stream that flew backwards six or seven feet before hitting the ground. Finally, he lowered his massive head and swung off among the trees, going about his business.

That business did eventually come to include killing men. Late in the afternoon of November 29, 1985, almost nine months after we left the park, a Nepalese laborer named Khan Bahadur was gathering firewood just a few yards from the Khinanoli rest house, in the heart of the forest. As Bahadur bent over, his arms already full of sticks, to retrieve one more, a tiger struck him from behind. He was dead before his load had clattered to the ground. The tiger dragged him into the undergrowth.

This time, Dhitu was clearly the culprit. His big, unmistakable pug marks—and only his—were found at the scene, and when the park director led a flotilla of ten elephants into the undergrowth a couple of hours after the attack, they found him crouching over the corpse, calmly eating. The tiger was as apparently contemptuous of human beings as ever; nothing Asok Singh and his men could think to do would drive him off his kill. Finally, he worked up enough of a thirst to go for water on his own, allowing the forest guards on elephants time to surround and recover what was left of the body.

Four days later, Brijendra Singh trapped the tiger in a steel cage. Dhitu now resides in the Kanpur zoo, where his reluctant captor has recently been to visit him. The tiger has sired two cubs since his incarceration and is "quite happy," Brijendra Singh says, "getting lots of meat." —GEOFFREY C. WARD

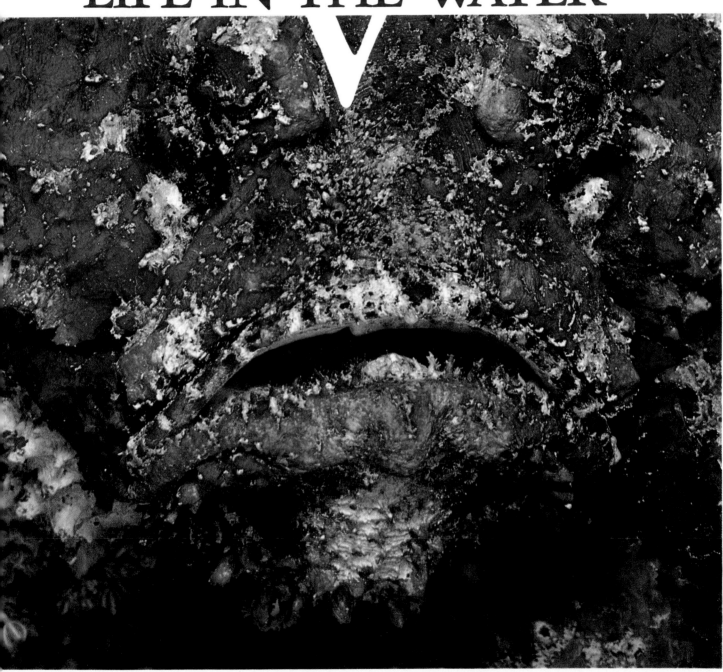

V
LIFE IN THE WATER

STATE OF THE REEF

TEXT BY KENNETH BROWER

For a newcomer to the coral reef, there is always a moment of vertigo. Part of the sensation, for divers, may be in the inner ear, which must make its adjustments to weightlessness and the pressure on the drum. But most of the dis-equilibrium, I think, is in the optic nerve and brain. The eye struggles to make sense of the confusions of color, motion, and shape that assault it. Nothing in the temperate zone can prepare the retina, or the mind behind, for what goes on under the surface of shallow tropical seas.

Last winter—the southern summer—after several years away in northern latitudes, I spent six weeks diving on the Great Barrier Reef. My eye, in its time away, had once again grown virginal. On my first dive it was as dismayed as it had ever been. I saw:

An angelfish, its yellow face all reticulated in electric blue, as if struck and filigreed just now by lightning. A cloud of fairy basslets, neon-pink. A school of blue-green parrotfish, turning in unison, opalescing as they caught the light. A pair of clown anemonefish, their orange bodies banded in greasepaint of a luminescent, lavender-tinted white; clowns lost in symbiotic love for their anemone, backing, bellying, diving, nuzzling, finning, rolling in the tentacles. A harlequin tuskfish, banded in red-orange and cobalt, fangs glowing a pale-blue, as if they were radioactive.

Hard corals. Soft corals. Fire corals. Lace corals. Bead corals. Button corals. Bubble corals. Vase corals. Organ-pipe corals. Wire corals. Staghorn corals. Rugose corals.

Mushroom corals, *Fungia,* their corallites folded like the gills on the underside of a mushroom. Plate corals, *Acropora hyacinthus,* made like giant hyacinths of stone. Brain corals, *Porites,* convoluted like the surface of the cerebral cortex. Where the

Far left: A sport diver and soft coral on Australia's Ribbon Reef.

Kinid Reef in Palau, Micronesia.

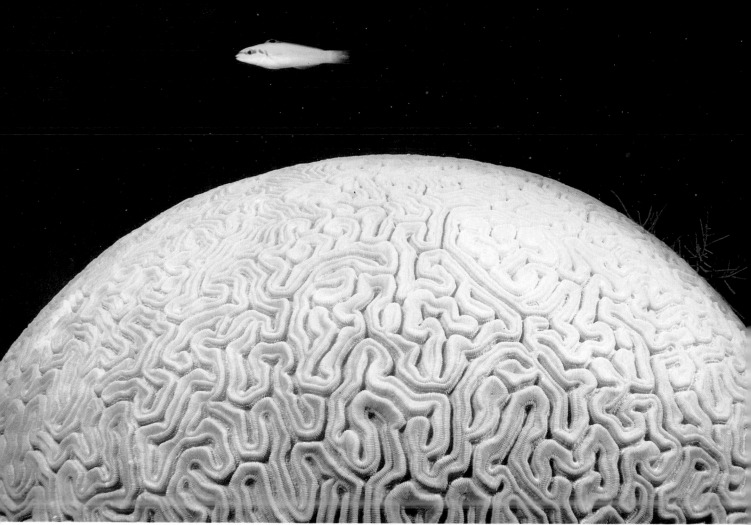

ABOVE: FRANKLIN VIOLA (COMSTOCK)
BELOW: STEPHAN MYERS

The patterns and textures produced by corals are, if anything, even more fascinating than their shapes and colors. A yellow-phase bluehead cruises over a grooved brain at Grand Cayman in the Caribbean, while two cleaning gobies graze a cavernous brain coral at Cozumel, Mexico. Far right photo: a mushroom coral at Palau in the Caroline Islands.

132

convolutions of our own brains are packed with neurons—memories, intuitions, bright ideas, telephone numbers—the convolutions of brain corals are packed with polyps. Brain corals are nocturnal ruminators; the polyps come out to wave their translucent tentacles at night.

Sea pens. Sea whips. Sea fans. Sea whips and fans are gorgonian corals. The whips grow straight or corkscrewed out from the coral wall. More often than not, each one is inhabited by a goby or a pair of them— small, translucent, desperately loyal fish. A goby cannot be chased away from its whip; the fish would rather die than leave it. The goby is forever flitting around to the other side, like a squirrel on a trunk. Sea fans spread themselves at right angles to the current, feeding on plankton. They have a wonderful two-dimensionality. They are like huge, lobate leaves pressed between the pages of a book, then forgotten there, nothing left but the veins.

A school of orange-spot surgeonfish came my way, each one dark-bodied with a daub of orange at the shoulder. They passed like reproductions of a single 1950s abstraction. The daubs of orange were laid on as if by brush, thick where they began at the shoulder, thinning tailward to show the texture of scales underneath, just as a brushstroke in

drying shows the texture of canvas. Orange spots danced before my eyes, as if from a blow to the head. Only as the last of them cleared did I see that the surgeonfish were not reproductions. They made a series. Each fish was an original. Neptune had loaded his brush a little differently in marking each one.

Several cornetfish hung horizontal and motionless in the middle distance. There is something unreal about cornetfish. Where most reef fish have short, deep profiles, the cornetfish's is long and low—an arrow of a fish. Where most reef fish are bright and polychromatic, the cornetfish is a dull monochrome. Where other reef fish swing with the surge, cornetfish seem magically immune to turbulence. The currents and cavitations of the reef somehow pass through without shifting them. There is a certain *trompe-l'oeil* to cornetfish. They are like warp threads missing from the bright woof of the reef. I imagined I could see through them to a drabber universe on the other side.

There were infinities in all directions. Coral reefs are the largest structures assembled by life on Earth, and this system, the greatest reef of all, stretched away a thousand miles to the southwest—if not an infinite distance, technically, then certainly a long way. A high proportion of reef species were

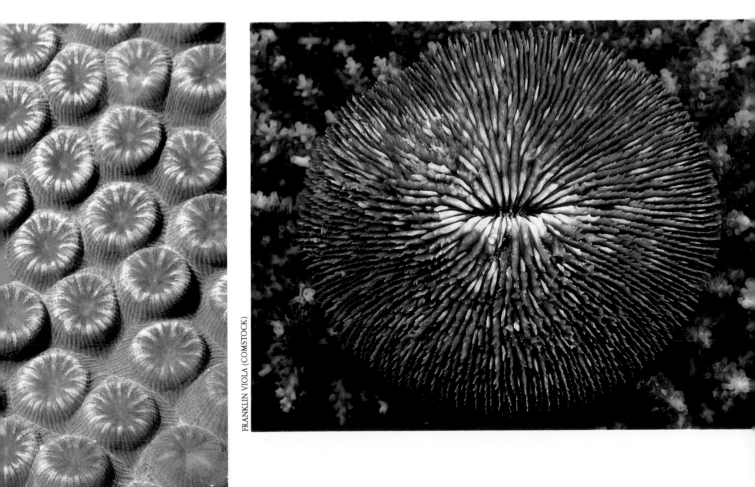

FRANKLIN VIOLA (COMSTOCK)

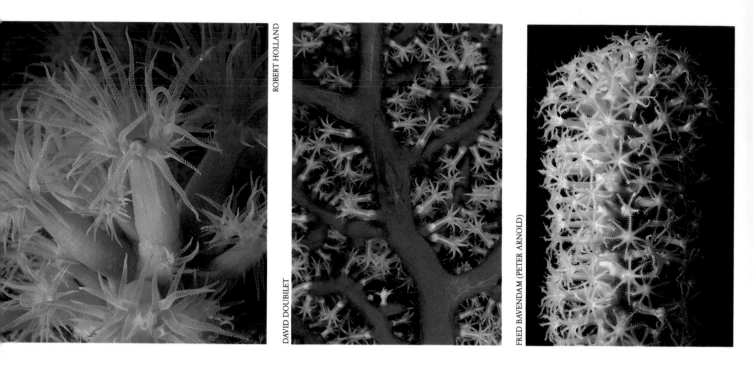

ROBERT HOLLAND

DAVID DOUBILET

FRED BAVENDAM (PETER ARNOLD)

Above: With polyps extended for feeding, many corals and gorgonians appear to have sprouted blossoms. And like garden plants, corals and their polyps exhibit a dazzling variety of shapes and colors.

There are few swimmers, men or women, in Kenya's Kikuyu tribe. Nyawira Muthiga (right) is a skilled diver and marine biologist who is studying a destructive infestation of sea urchins on coral reefs off Kenya's Indian Ocean coast.

still unknown to science—if not numberless, then unnumbered. And if the macrocosm extended nearly forever, then so did the microcosm. On the coral head beside me lived a clam, and on the clam lived a sponge, and on the sponge a tiny red mite, and on the mite—what? The old reef vertigo was upon me.

Nyawira Muthiga stood on the reef at Diani, off Kenya's coast. The coral under her feet was dead. Nothing prospered around her but sea urchins.

Muthiga is a young Kikuyu woman, slender, beautiful, six feet tall. She wears her hair in French braids tight against her skull, then tied behind in a bun. The subjects of her transect, the urchins, had evolved the opposite sort of coiffure. Their spines stuck out stiffly all over. It was a proliferation of urchins that had killed stretches of the Diani reef and depauperized the rest. The urchins made a plague as devastating, in its way, as any plague of locusts on the African mainland.

Nyawira Muthiga is the rarest of creatures, a Kikuyu female marine biologist. There are few swimmers in her tribe, let alone women swimmers, let alone women divers. Muthiga is not just a diver but a "ham" in the water, according to a colleague who has watched her work. "When I was in school in Florida, there were always field trips to national parks," Muthiga told me. "I wasn't interested. I had been to all the parks in Kenya— elephants, rhinos. But trips to the ocean! *That* was different."

She and her American husband, Timothy McClanahan, are in the middle of a study of Kenya's sea-urchin infestation. In the lagoon off Diani, the biomass of urchins has increased fivefold since 1970. The biggest population explosion has been in *Echinometra mathaei,* the smallest of the reef's three species of sea urchin. *E. mathaei* is a solitary, short-spined creature that normally lives in burrows it excavates by feeding on coral and by wire-brushing the coral substrate with its spines. As its numbers have boomed, the little urchin has forsaken its natural habitat, departing the burrows to forage everywhere on the lagoon floor.

When their numbers are in balance, scraping and boring organisms like *E. mathaei* are a dynamic force on the reef, varying the topography of the substrate, diversifying life. Multiplying out of balance, they break down the reef faster than the corals can build it. The urchin is wildly out of balance off Kenya. A decent enough creature in normal circumstances, it has become a kind of monster.

Jeremy Jackson stood on the reef at Bahia Las Minas, on the Caribbean coast of Panama. The subtidal corals beneath him displayed a startling array of injuries. Some were bleached, others were producing inordinate amounts of mucus. In some, the tissues were swelling, in others tissues had sloughed.

Jackson is a tall man—an inch or two taller than Nyawira Muthiga—and as fair-skinned as she is dark. His auburn hair was not *ar-*

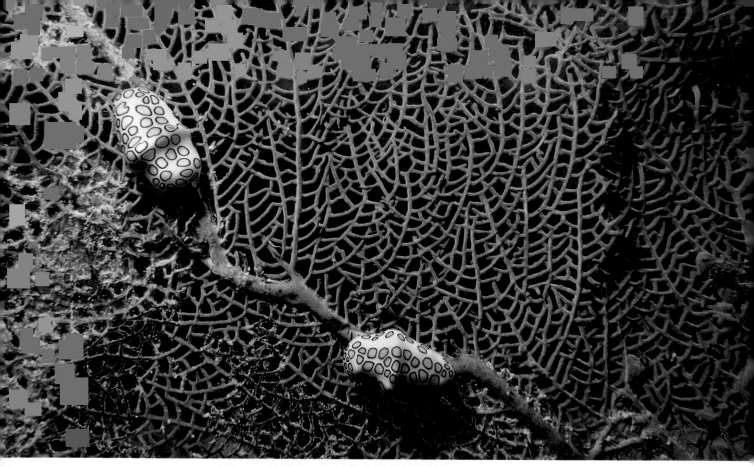

ABOVE: BOYD NORTON. BELOW: FRED BAVENDAM (PETER ARNOLD)

Diving on a Carribean coral reef is a little like visiting a museum of modern art; the shapes and colors, and textures of its inhabitants are wonderfully rich and varied. Even the names delight: above, flamingo tongues on a seafan; below, a feathered Christmas tree worm over a depressed brain coral. At top right, an orange sea lily, and below right, a red finger sponge.

ranged in any way; it was phenomenal, expanding like a nova or a hedge gone wild. It is the sort of hair we expect in our physicists and composers, not in our marine biologists. Jackson is a marine biologist indeed, at the Smithsonian Tropical Research Institute in Panama. Fate had just presented him with a scientific problem he'd just as soon have done without. The previous month more than eight million liters of Mexican–Venezuelan crude oil had spilled from a ruptured refinery storage tank at the bay.

"The spill occurred at a time of exceptionally low tides, and for that reason the oil was dammed up along the crest of the reef," he says. "That's also the reason so much of it stayed in the mangroves. They sprayed twenty thousand liters of dispersant to try to make the problem appear to go away. It didn't work. The oil killed mangroves along a hundred kilometers of coast in the bay. It killed corals all along the reef crest."

The oil's destruction of intertidal corals on the reef flat was nothing new. Even the oil companies admit that oil kills shallow-water corals. What was new was the wounds on subtidal corals. Until now most marine scientists had considered subtidal coral to be more or less immune to oil. Before Bahia Las Minas, most tropical oil spills had occurred on stretches of coast where no scientific observations had been made. The Panama spill was different—a fortunate calamity—in that sites within the bay had been subject to a fifteen-year monitoring program. Jackson organized a $3 million, five-year, twenty-man study of the spill.

Jeremy Jackson has a deep, carrying baritone. When describing the difficulty of teasing statistical significance from oil-spill data, he hurries through the details in an obligatory way, and the baritone gets louder with impatience and frustration. If he had his choice, Jackson would not be studying spilled oil at all. "It's very disruptive," he told me. "It screws up your life. All of a sudden you have to spend all your time working on something you're not even necessarily interested in. I've never worked in pollution biology before. I must say it's not what interests me most."

Comparing the number of coral colonies, before and after the spill, was a "mess," he says. No trend manifested itself. The *size* of colonies showed a clearer pattern, dropping markedly right after the spill, but not in a way that was statistically significant. Comparing the extent of coral cover, before and after, proved problematical, too. "Natural communities are so extraordinarily patchy that you need a vast amount of information in order to be able to separate the signal from the noise," he says. "No signal, no oil effect—and oil companies love you, because you didn't find anything." A comparison of the growth of colonies, before and after, had the same signal-to-noise problem. What did work for Jackson and his colleagues was a survey of coral wounds.

"Incidence of injuries was a much more satisfying thing to look at," he says, a little ghoulishly. He and his co-workers pioneered a system for measuring reef damage by a survey of injuries. "They're quick and dirty," he says of the surveys. "You can do a reef in a few hours, you get an enormous amount of data, and it really shows an effect." The effect shown in the Bahia Las Minas is that spills are profoundly injurious to subtidal corals. Reefs are not protected by depth of water over them. Oil is even worse for corals than we thought. The reefs of the world grow, unfortunately, in the latitudes where most of the oil lies. On the fate of the reefs, Jackson has joined a growing army of Jeremiahs.

Robert Endean stood at the lectern at James Cook University, in Townsville, Australia, in August 1987. He was a few miles inshore of the Great Barrier Reef. Projected on a screen behind Endean was a slide of a massive coral, bone-white and dead. The lecture hall was jammed. Endean was addressing the Sixth International Coral Reef Symposium,

BOTH: STEPHAN MYERS

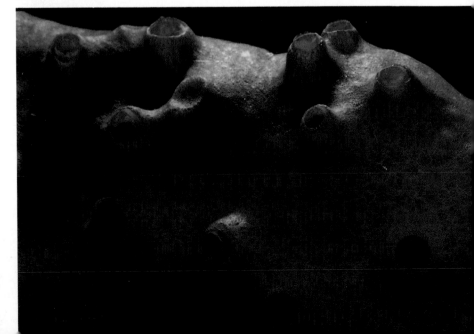

attended by more than 700 coral-reef specialists from around the world. Most of those 700 scientists seemed to have crowded into this particular session. Standees lined the back of the room, and others sat in the aisles.

Of the prophets of doom for coral reefs, Robert Endean is the most stentorian. He is a zoology professor at the University of Queensland, and for twenty years he has been a student of *Acanthaster planci*, the crown-of-thorns starfish. In part from the Biblical force of its name, in part from Endean's tireless rhetoric against the starfish, in part from its eerie familiarity from science-fiction horror movies, and largely because of its very real and widespread depredations on Pacific reefs, *Acanthaster planci* has become the symbol for coral-reef destruction everywhere.

The first outbreak of *Acanthaster*—the first to be detected by modern man, at any rate—came in the 1960s. In that decade the starfish destroyed large tracts of reef in Australia, the Philippines, Okinawa, Taiwan, Thailand, New Guinea, the Solomons, Samoa, Tahiti, and in Guam and Palau and other archipelagoes of Micronesia. Robert Endean prophesied that *Acanthaster*, if unchecked, would destroy the Great Barrier Reef entirely.

Endean is a prophet without a lot of honor in his own profession. He has a little of the look and delivery of an Outback snake-oil salesman, and many of his colleagues dismiss him as being just that.

Few marine scientists believe the crown-of-thorns is a creature quite so apocalyptic as Endean claims. Almost none accept his theory of how the starfish went wrong. (Endean believes that human collecting of the shells of the giant triton, one of the few known predators on adult crown-of-thorns starfish, has allowed *Acanthaster* to multiply out of control.) Endean's opponents make strong arguments that predation on *adult* starfish is not likely to be limiting. They point to clear evidence for outbreaks of *Acanthaster* in the fossil record, before man could have figured in the equation. They insist that reefs devastated by the crown-of-thorns have shown a remarkable recovery.

Many reef scientists, both friends and foes of Endean, have trouble with his science. The banners of his crusade, they believe, wave everywhere in his methodology. But whatever his colleagues say about him, they cannot deny that Endean is a draw among them. He can fill a lecture hall. This day, the fifth and last day of the symposium, there was an electricity in the auditorium that had been missing from all previous sessions. Scientists like human drama, too. There promised to be a fight, and they had come, I guessed, for that.

The title of Endean's paper, "*Acanthaster planci* Predation on Massive Corals: The Myth of Rapid Recovery of Devastated Reefs," was typically contentious. Endean and his coauthors had compared three reefs that had suffered heavy infestations of starfish with three reefs that had not. They found that colony density of massive corals was markedly lower on infested reefs. Two-thirds of the surviving massive corals on infested reefs had suffered extensive tissue loss. More than half of the surviving massive corals, they estimated, could be expected to succumb to overgrowth by soft corals, or to predation by residual populations of the crown-of-thorns.

"Several decades," Endean said, in summing up, "and probably more than a century, will be required for the densities and size structures of colonies of massive corals typical of those found on reefs unaffected by *Acanthaster planci* to be attained. This assumes that no further outbreaks will occur during the recovery phase.

"If *Acanthaster planci* outbreaks occur as soon as the cover of rapidly growing branching corals is established—this requires about fifteen years after the first outbreak—on numerous reefs, then massive corals are heading for local extinction on reefs in the central third of the Great Barrier Reef, and in the long term perhaps centuries-long impoverishment of these reefs is possible."

Endean seemed tired. He spoke with plenty of conviction, but without the passion of a man seeking to engage his audience—not any longer. Voices in the wilderness must sometimes grow hoarse.

"It is apparent that rapid recovery of reefs devastated by *Acanthaster planci* has not occurred," Endean concluded. "Indeed, rapid recovery of reefs devastated by *Acanthaster planci* seems to be a myth. Thank you."

The moderator asked for questions. No hands went up. There was a moment of silence, then a murmur of incredulity traveled the auditorium. We all knew a number of biologists in this room who had publicly challenged several of the assertions Endean had just made. We knew biologists here who supported Endean and would have challenged the counter-assertions. But if the scientists had come for a fight, as I had guessed, then they had lost enthusiasm. Twenty years of bitter argument on the crown-of-thorns had been enough, it seemed. I sensed some kind of collective *Aw, what the hell*. Several hundred reef scientists, realizing there were to be no questions—not a single one—looked at one another in amazement. People began to chuckle, and the whole auditorium softly laughed.

In the Indian Ocean, coral reefs are dying off Tanzania. Tanzanian resort beaches formerly protected by the rampart of the reef are now eroding at a rate of five meters per year. Off Madagascar, reefs and mangrove forests are disappearing fast. Off the southwest coast of Sri Lanka—the island that plays Madagascar to the subcontinent of India—reefs are being mined for limestone. The natural barrier that protected Sri Lanka's coast has sprung gaps, and monsoon waves are eroding the shore. The science-fiction writer Arthur C. Clarke, a resident of Sri Lanka and a diver, has suggested that in a few decades we might see a "Separation of Sri Lanka," the split beginning at the southwest corner of the island. Should this come to pass, the separated corner would play Sri Lanka to Sri Lanka. The separation may prove to be just more science fiction, but Clarke has been right in his science fiction before.

In the Caribbean, in the summer of 1987, corals on many reefs went white. This "coral bleaching" seems to have been associated

Controversial University of Queensland zoology professor Robert Endean has studied the crown-of-thorns starfish for twenty years and prophesies that it will destroy the Great Barrier Reef if its depredations are not halted. But few of his colleagues believe that the creature is quite so apocalyptic as Endean claims. Many Pacific reefs devastated by the starfish, scientists say, have made remarkable recoveries.

with water temperatures higher than usual. The Caribbean may simply have suffered one bad year, of course, but scientists wonder. There is some speculation that the blanched corals may have seen a ghost—the specter of the Greenhouse Effect and global warming.

In the Pacific, the millennial event, or perhaps the 200-year event—if one of those is what *Acanthaster planci* represents—now seems to be occurring every fifteen years.

A report on the health of the world's reefs—a State of the Reef Message—is not easy to formulate. We know little about how coral communities are supposed to be, and it is hard to be sure when something is wrong with them.

Western science has come very late to tropical reefs. The first great reef biologist was Charles Darwin. In the century and a half since Darwin deduced, correctly, the manner in which coral atolls form, we have only begun to catalog the reef's inhabitants, to unravel the reef's webs of interdependency, to measure its cycles, to guess at its workings. The coral reef has been called "The Ultimate Ecosystem." There is no more complex natural community on the face of the planet, unless it is tropical forest. If the eye of the diver suffers its moments of vertigo in contemplating the reef, then so does the eye of science.

"One of the problems is that we are terrestrial animals," Richard Kenchington, a biologist at the Great Barrier Reef Marine Park Authority, told me last summer. "We tend to look at a coral reef, which is a complex biological structure, and think, 'Ah, I understand this, because I know what it's like to walk in a woodland.' In the old days people were making comparisons between coral reefs and redwood forests. They were looking at massive corals and saying, 'Those are hundreds of years old, therefore it works like a redwood forest.' But the thing about the terrestrial system is that your long-lived major dominants modify the whole rest of the environment. That's not so true on the reef. There's not a lot of dynamics in a forest, compared to a coral reef."

The first scientists to see corals mistook them for plants. The next generation, the scientists of Darwin's time, were amused by this error, having come themselves to the certainty that corals were animals. Scientists of the twentieth century have thrown things back into ambiguity. They have discovered that all reef-building corals harbor small algae, called zooxanthellae, in their tissues. The planktonic organisms snatched by polyp tentacles are really just snacks. Most of the food on which corals live, and most of the fuel on which they build the great cities of their reefs, is produced by photosynthesis in zooxanthellae.

Are corals animals that farm algae in their tissues? Or are corals, in their staggering diversity (plates, vases, buttons, bubbles, brains, fans, whips, staghorns, thousands of shapes and species), just a simple alga's ingenious way of elaborating palaces for itself?

We are in the middle of a revolution in our way of looking at the reef. Ten years ago it was commonplace to speak of coral reefs as "fragile." Tropical marine organisms live at temperatures closer to their upper thermal limits than do temperate organisms; they live closer to their lower oxygen limits; they require clear water and are sensitive to the smallest increases in turbidity. The dead reefs in the wake of the crown-of-thorns, the demise of reefs in sedimental places like Hawaii's Kaneohe Bay, did indeed make it seem that reefs are delicate systems. It now appears that they are tougher and more resilient than we thought.

"What we see from the crown-of-thorns, and from cyclone damage, is that you can get major changes of communities and relative abundances in very short periods," Richard Kenchington told me. "People will say, after a crown-of-thorns outbreak, 'Oh, that reef's stuffed, it's finished.' You go out and have a look seven or eight years later, and you're sure you're at the wrong reef. You're surrounded by beautiful corals."

"You get discouraged," Charles Birkeland of the University of Guam told me, in describing a starfish-damaged reef he has been monitoring in American Samoa. "You go back every three years and the reef is dead. Then one time you go back and the reef is there."

"It's a straight mathematical problem of doubling time," Kenchington explains. "Even a fast-growing colony, one of those which is doubling its mass every twelve months, has to start off from pinhead size. You have to go through a few years before that pinhead becomes fist-sized. Once it becomes fist-sized, then it doesn't take long before you've got a really big coral. Through the first seven years, the place does look desolate, and yet if you get down on your hands and knees and really look closely, you see there are thirty or forty colonies per square meter. Sometimes as many as three hundred colonies per square meter."

Until recently, the coral reef was regarded as a stable and benign environment in which populations were more or less in equilibrium. This was mostly an intuition, based on little more than thermometer readings.

(In temperature, at least, tropical seas do fluctuate less than do the seas of higher latitudes.) Boom-and-bust economies were supposed to be features of high-latitude places like the Arctic, places with simplified ecosystems. The coral reef, with all the checks and balances of its intricate food chains, all the bet-hedging inherent in its complexity, was supposed to be immune to the feasts and famines that characterize the North. Lemmings and voles cyclically overrun their boreal habitat, not rabbitfish and squirrelfish. Or so we thought. Scientists are now overhauling the generalization.

"Large changes occur all the time, on lots of reefs, *independently of whatever it is you want to study,*" Jeremy Jackson warns.

Populations of sea urchins are booming now off Kenya, but in 1983 urchin populations collapsed off the Caribbean coasts of Panama and Columbia, where disease killed 99 percent of the *Diadema antillarum.* In 1982 populations of *Echinothrix* urchins went bust in Hawaii's windward islands. Epidemics have repeatedly decimated sponge populations in the Caribbean and the Gulf of Mexico. In 1983, and again in 1985, there was mass mortality of coral in the eastern Pacific. Black-band disease, white-band disease, white-wasting disease, and other epidemic maladies of coral have ravaged the populations in several seas. In 1983, 17 million seabirds disappeared from Christmas Island.

How are we to know which of these fluctuations are natural and which are caused by man? How, in light of our ignorance of the reefs, are we to manage and conserve them?

Despite the millions of Australian and American dollars that have gone into research on *Acanthaster planci,* the cause of outbreaks of the crown-of-thorns is still unknown. The starfish remains nearly as mysterious as some alien thing from the stars.

No one who writes on *Acanthaster* can avoid the science-fiction metaphor. The body plan is from a grade-B sci-fi movie—a spiny, many-armed disk, slow-moving but inexorable. There is something low-budget even in the color scheme—vague tans and purples applied without much skill. The spines are poisonous. The starfish can regenerate from parts of itself. (The natives of several archipelagoes overlooked this trait in early control efforts, when they tried to kill starfish by cutting them up. They succeeded only in seeding their reefs with dragon's teeth.) The starfish has manners as horrible as any movie beast's, everting its stomach through its mouth to envelope coral with its digestive system. Feeding, crowns-of-thorns release

SANDRO TUCCI (BLACK STAR)

chemicals that attract more crowns-of-thorns. They attack the reef en masse, forming fronts, mats, moving in a sort of glacial feeding frenzy—the Blob with spines. *Acanthaster* even has in Robert Endean its offbeat scientist who sees the danger before anyone and tries to alert a complacent world.

The great dither of human scientists over the menace of *Acanthaster planci* is amusing, in a way. As a threat to coral reefs, the crown-of-thorns, for all its movie-monster spines, has nothing on *Homo sapiens.* The real plague on the reef is man.

The plague on the reef is rich men. In the Caribbean, the anchors and mooring lines of yachts do considerable damage to corals. Drifting lobster traps—lost by Caribbean fishermen who could never afford to eat their own catch—go ghost-fishing among the corals. Monofilament fishing line garrotes coral heads, and scuba divers vacationing from high latitudes step on them. In the Caribbean especially, but in other seas as well, the construction of resort hotels near the reef produces siltation, and the operation of those hotels generates effluents that are harmful to coral.

In January last year, from a coastal road in Queensland, I looked—then looked again—

American scientist John McManus, of the Marine Science Institute at the University of the Philippines, watches over his research reefs with aid of an ultralight airplane.

BOTH: LYNN FUNKHOUSER (PETER ARNOLD)

at a flat-topped island moving slowly along the Coral Sea horizon. The apparition might have been Gulliver's Laputa, come to life and flying low. It was not, of course; it was the Four Seasons Barrier Reef floating hotel. I watched, with a sinking feeling, as it made its way south from Singapore to its permanent anchorage on the Great Barrier Reef near Townsville.

The hotel is the first of its kind. Its seven stories and 200 rooms will accommodate short-staying tourists—most of them American, according to the promoters—with room prices ranging from $340 to $820 a day.

The distant mesa of the Four Seasons was moving beyond the two humps of Double Island, discovered and named by Captain Cook. What would Cook have made of this, I wondered? Would the captain of *Endeavor* have believed *Mighty Servant 2*, the Dutch heavy-lift vessel that towed the hotel? Would he have believed a 12,000-ton floating hotel on the reefs that so nearly wrecked him just two centuries ago?

The floating hotel's destination was John Brewer Reef. John Brewer is, after Green Island, the Australian reef hardest hit by the crown-of-thorns predation in the last two outbreaks of the starfish.

Giant clams of the genus Tridacna *(left) are on their way to extinction on many Indo-Pacific reefs because of depredations by Taiwanese poachers. To supply the aquarium-fish trade, Filipino collectors squirt cyanide from detergent bottles (top), but for every fish captured alive in a plastic bag, nine others die.*

143

Beauty is in the eye of the beholder—and the beheld—as these Caribbean fishes attest: a queen angelfish (top left), scrawled tilefish (top right), porcupinefish (above), and a coney (bottom right) in its gaudiest colors.

The plague on the reef is poor men. Most of the planet's reefs are in the Third World; reef destruction is largely a problem of undeveloped nations.

The reefs of the Philippines are the most diverse in the world, and the most threatened. Philippine reefs support more than 2,000 species of fish (the Great Barrier Reef, for comparison, supports around 1,500), yet a recent study of 619 Philippine reefs showed that 70 percent were dead or dying. The islands inshore of these most prolific of the planet's reefs are also prolific—too prolific of humans.

Dredging, fishing with dynamite, coral and shell collecting, and the aquarium fish trade are all destroying coral communities throughout the archipelago. The fish-dynamiters are poor men destroying their children's future in order to feed them today. The aquarium-fish collectors are poor men who dive in fins cut from plywood, breathing from hookah hoses stuck in their mouths, and carrying small detergent bottles refilled with sodium cyanide. The divers call the chemical "magic."

A squirt into the coral, and all the fish hiding there come out spinning and jerking. Any angelfish, triggerfish, squirrelfish, or blue tangs the diver catches in his hand. Most of the rest are unmarketable and left spiraling and fluttering amid poisoned corals. For every fish captured alive by cyanide, nine die, by the estimate of Steve Robinson of the International Marinelife Alliance. "Magic" is black magic. Cyanide fishing is an effective method in the short term, disastrous in the long. The chemical is bad for the health of the divers, who suffer skin lesions and hair loss and sometimes fatally poison themselves; bad for the longevity of the cyanide-shocked fish; and fatal for the coral upon which the aquarium-fish business—and millions of Filipinos—depend.

In Madagascar, as in the Philippines, the linked problems of poverty and human numbers are decimating reefs. Twenty-five years ago the reefs of Madagascar's Tuléar Region were pristine. Since then a population boom and unemployment have hit the coast. Fish consumption has doubled in the past fifteen years. There has been a sharp decline in the size of fish caught. Diversity has decreased 50 percent in some fish families. The mangrove forest, nursery for many reef species, has almost entirely disappeared, logged for charcoal. Erosion has followed widespread deforestation inland, with consequent siltation of reefs. Garbage is dumped on the Tuléar beaches, and at low tide the shoreline becomes a latrine. Eutrophication is causing algal blooms on the reef, and infestations of *Diadema* urchins have followed.

The plague on the reef is Chinese. Giant clams, genus *Tridacna,* are just a memory on the reefs of China, a consequence not so much of human poverty and numbers—though China can certainly boast those—as of passionate, gastronomic cravings for the exotic. ("Would you like to eat *forbidden* things?" Paul Theroux's Chinese guide whispers, in Theroux's fine report on this syndrome.) Their own reef larder looted, Southeast Asian clammers moved outward into the western Indo–Pacific. As the big clams disappeared from those waters too, the clammers

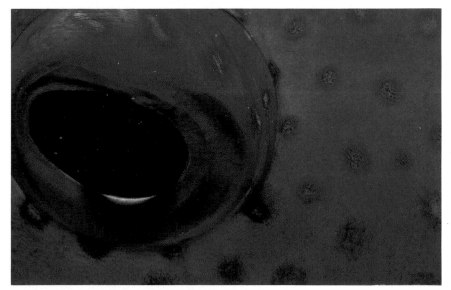

pushed east. In Fiji the giant clams are on their way to extinction, largely because of the depredations of the Taiwanese. Stocks of big clams of several species have declined precipitously on reefs near inhabited Fijian islands, where they are collected and eaten by Fijians, but they are plummeting also on uninhabited reefs, where they are falling prey to Taiwanese poachers.

"In recent years two Taiwanese clam vessels have been apprehended in Fijian waters and several others sighted," Sue Wells reports in

Species, the newsletter of the Species Survival Commission. "The diary of a Taiwanese skipper, confiscated during an incident in Australian waters, concluded with the observation that 'reefs to the north of Australia and east at least as far as Fiji have been fished out—the only place with clams of any size and quantity is Australia.' As a Fiji Fisheries Department officer commented, 'There you have it—straight from the pen of one of the most experienced field surveyors in the Pacific.' "

The giant of giant clams, *Tridacna gigas,* is very rare or extinct in Fiji. The last known living specimen was taken fifteen years ago.

The plague on the reef is Japanese. One of the last undisturbed coral reefs of the Okinawa region, Shiraho Reef of Ishigaki Island, in the Ryukyu chain, is threatened by airport construction. Shiraho's fishermen have protested the airport, as have fifty-six other Japanese groups, among them the Okinawa Committee of 100 for Peace, the Shiraho People's Airport Opposition Committee, the Japan Nature Conservation Society, the Adan Society, Friends of the Earth Japan, labor unions, church groups, consumer organizations, women's groups, teachers' associations, and Jacques Cousteau besides; but in modern Japan none of this amounts to clout. Plans for the airport are proceeding. The proponents promise to build a "coral museum" on the paved-over reef.

The plague on the reef is Africans. Of the seven Tanzanian reefs recently recommended for World Heritage status, five are now dead, blasted by Tanzanian fish-dynamiters. The plague is Indonesians and Polynesians and Melanesians. Island peoples were once fine stewards of their reefs, but with Westernization the old management skills and sensibilities are departing. The plague is any of us with a spear gun and scuba gear in his closet, as I have in mine, or a cowrie on his desk, like the cowrie staring me in the face right now.

Those "natural" plagues on many reefs may prove to be unnatural in the end. If Nyawira Muthiga and Timothy McClanahan are right in their speculations, the sea urchins infesting Kenya's reefs are secondary agents, an epiphenomenon. The first agent and phenomenon is man. The beach at Diani, off which the urchins are multiplying fastest, is the most developed tourist beach in Kenya, and one of the most heavily fished. What has happened, Muthiga and McClanahan believe, is that some "keystone" predator—its identity as yet unknown—has been eliminated by overfishing or pollution.

The prospects are bleak, but not entirely.

"A reef *will* regrow again, if you leave it alone," Sue Wells told me. Wells, an Englishwoman, is editor of a massive, three-volume inventory, *Coral Reefs of the World,* recently published by the International Union for Conservation of Nature and Natural Resources. Her inventory was five years in the making, and her antennae, her network of reefwise correspondents, cover all the tropics. If anyone has a sense of the state of the reefs, it is she. "I worry about Madagascar," she said. "I feel good about Oman. I feel good about the cooperative programs in Southeast Asia. I felt good about Fiji, when things were really beginning to move there. I don't feel so good about Fiji anymore. But I'm confident about a lot of Pacific atolls.

"Tom Vant Hof, who has been working in the Caribbean, is very pessimistic. He gives the reefs only a couple of years. I wouldn't be that pessimistic, just because I think there's an incredible *will* to do something about it."

One new approach to reef conservation has been the suggestion that we return to old approaches. The principal spokesman for this school is Robert Johannes, an expatriate Canadian marine biologist who presently lives and works in Tasmania. Johannes has studied traditional fishing knowledge and reef management in Palau, the Torres Strait, and the Solomon Islands.

"Pacific Islanders invented all the basic fisheries conservation measures," Johannes told me recently. "The measures that we invented about ninety years ago, they invented hundreds of years ago—limited entry, closed areas, closed seasons, restrictions on fishing gear."

Marjorie Falanruw, a biologist from the Micronesian archipelago of Yap, argues for a resurrection of the old environmental ethic of Oceania. She speaks of "neotraditions." The shamans of Yap, she points out, are a species of environmentalist. She suggests that what the islands need are *neo*shamans, men and women with roots in the old wisdom and branches in the new. Parks and resource policies designed by such people would draw on all 40,000 years of human knowledge of the Pacific, not just the tail end of it. It's a radical notion, but one the reefs might live with: that the seeds of the future lie in the past.

There are promising modern developments as well. The Great Barrier Reef Marine Park, established by act of the Australian Commonwealth in 1975, is, many think, the best thing to happen to reefs since zooxanthellae. Marine-park planners all across the tropics are looking toward that great park for example. At present, 2,100 reef complexes and most of the 1,250-mile length of the Great Barrier Reef are given one form of protection or another. The basic tenet of the park's planners is that they will manage people, not ecosystems. This is a wise and appropriately humble first principle. The reef ecosystem is too complex for human tinkering and will be left to take care of itself.

Management is through an intricate zoning system: General Use "A" zones (where prawn trawling is permitted), General Use "B" (where trawling is not), Marine National Park "A" and "B" zones, scientific-research zones, preservation zones, replenishment areas, seasonal-closure areas. The system is overseen by a somewhat bewildering assortment of agencies: the Great Barrier Reef Marine Park Authority (GBRMPA), the Queensland National Parks and Wildlife Service, and the Queensland Fisheries Service among them. In Australia it seems to work.

How well it will work in the Third World, where most reefs lie, and where nations are far less wealthy and educated, is a question

asked by many reef scientists. I put it to Richard Kenchington of GBRMPA this summer.

"We are not an ideal model, because we had absolutely everything going for us," he answered. "We had strong public support for the concept that the reef is precious, fragile, and in need of protection. We also had the incomparable advantage of a piece of legislation which gives us legislative superiority over virtually every other act of Parliament. Our legislation allows us to overrule Defense, unless we're actually at war."

Many tropical nations have much less than absolutely everything going for them, of course. More often they have something like the opposite. And in the Third World, park people do not overrule defense agencies; it invariably works the other way around. Edgardo Gomez of the Philippines speaks of the "general problem" of his country's reefs—an illegal fishing boat or piece of extractive technology owned by a general. In Fiji, after the 1987 coup, the Fijian army confiscated Fisheries Department boats and pressed them into service as collecting ves-

Reef fishes have evolved many ways to protect themselves. Some species such as this stoplight parrotfish in the Caymans— surround themselves in a mucous cocoon at night.

ROBERT HOLLAND

Old hands in the reef business—fisheries officers, wardens, marine biologists—all seem to have a favorite one of these places. Once or twice in a lifetime, some obscure business takes the reef man there, and he never forgets. The first thing that strikes him, generally, is the size and number of the giant clams. *Tridacna gigas* is the emblem of unspoiled reef; its numbers seem to occur in inverse proportion to those of *Homo sapiens*. The next thing that strikes the reef man is the size and tameness of the fishes.

For Robert Owen, former chief conservationist of the Trust Territory of the Pacific Islands, that place is Helen Reef, an uninhabited outlier of the Southwest Islands, themselves distant outliers of the Palau Archipelago. In Owen's accounts, Helen Reef has that almost mythical plenteousness that Kentucky or the Great Plains held in the tales of the first white men to see them.

For Bill Pululoa, a fisheries officer in the Marshall Islands, that place is a Marshallese atoll called Bikar. "The atoll is full of sharks, but they don't bother you," Pululoa once told me. "On the lagoon bottom we saw these big coral heads. After a while, we noticed that they seemed to be following the boat. When the boat would stop, they would stop. They were big bumphead wrasse. You couldn't throw a lure overboard without instantly catching a fish. Big jacks were biting the props. One sheared the pin. We landed and looked around. As you walked along the beach, fish in the lagoon would follow you. When you stopped, they stopped."

These out-of-the-way reefs are reminders of what the tropical ocean was like before man; not just modern man and his supertankers and missile cruisers, but Stone Age man and the double canoes and outrigger canoes in which he colonized the warm seas.

There are now seventy marine protected areas in Indonesia and forty-two in Papua New Guinea—ambitious programs. In UNESCO's Man and the Biosphere Program there are presently eight biosphere reserves that include coral reefs. Four reefs have been declared World Heritage Sites. A good start.

But the great problem for marine protected areas, especially in the Third World, is enforcement. Tom Vant Hof, an officer of Saba Marine Park in the Netherlands Antilles, recently surveyed a number of Caribbean nations. There were, he found, species limits in the fishing regulations of 72 percent of the countries surveyed, size and weight limits in 78 percent, gear limits in 84 percent—and enforcement capability in just 19 percent. In the marine protected areas of the Caribbean, he found, only 31 percent had enforcement.

The anchors of pleasure boats cause inestimable damage to reefs, like this coral colony broken in half (facing page) on Australia's Great Barrier Reef. The grounding of a container ship in 1984 at Florida's Key Largo National Marine Sanctuary (above) left staghorn coral colonies in ruins.

sels, making the rounds of fishing villages in an attempt to boost production. The soldiers were not fish-handlers, and much of the catch spoiled. The Fijian army, on the heels of a study demonstrating a precipitous decline of Fiji's giant clams, contracted with the Taiwanese to supply a ton of giant-clam adductor muscle per month. Fiji's generals have entered into agreements to supply 140 tons of *bêche-de-mer* annually, from waters which until now have exported only forty to fifty tons a year.

Here and there in the tropical ocean, unmentioned in the mnemonic chants by which the old navigators learned their star courses, outside the compass routes of modern commerce, are reefs and islands missed by man.

In what sense exactly, one might ask, are the protected areas protected?

"There are elements of the model which can be tailored to other places," Richard Kenchington told me, of the example of the Great Barrier Reef Marine Park. "The central element is that we are managing people, not ecosystems. If your management doesn't provide to meet the needs of the people who are exploiting reefs, forget about it. You're not going to make it." Kenchington himself has recently made trips to the Galápagos Islands and to the Maldives, where he served as consultant to marine-park planners. The planners of both archipelagoes have been attentive.

"Most encouraging is the stuff that's being done in the Philippines," he said. "Building conservation up from the village level. Getting the people who go fishing to appreciate and understand a bit more about how the system ticks. Getting them to understand—admittedly, over a period of three, five, seven years of hard work with them—that by protecting an area they increase their fish take in surrounding areas."

The Philippine successes have proceeded from cooperative international programs like the Coastal Resources Management Project. They have been the work of native scientists like Angel Alcala and Edgardo Gomez, and of outsiders like John McManus and Steve Robinson.

John McManus, of the Marine Science Institute at the University of the Philippines, is an American who has begun to blend, like a Joseph Conrad character, into the fabric of his adopted islands. He is married to a Filipino woman. He is Filipino in build, as slender as any of the fishermen he works among. There is now something vaguely Filipino about his features. McManus is famous among colleagues for his reef overflights by ultralight aircraft, which he learned to fly as a way of cutting the high costs of aerial surveys. (Making more of less is a Filipino talent, and one crucial to a marine scientist working in the islands.) There is no question where McManus' loyalties lie: "People are judgmental when they hear about fish-dynamiting," he says. "Robin Hood got started when he went against the king's law. People were hungry when there was a lot of food around."

McManus emphasizes that there are huge differences between the schemes that work in Australia and those that will work in the Philippines. He believes that in the Philippines local coastal management makes more sense than national regulation. He proposes a village-based adaptive management system

ROBERT HOLLAND

LEN ZEIL

An extraordinarily low tide exposes a vast expanse of coral reef in Palau.

in which "environmental community organizers" are assigned to villages to evaluate the local fisheries resource, to study the local environment—natural, economic, and sociological—and to educate villagers as to their management options. Early experiments with such a system are working well.

Steve Robinson, while working as a clerk in a California aquarium store in the late 1960s, was mystified by the "junk" butterflyfish and angelfish from the Philippines. Why, he wondered, were Hawaiian fish so much hardier? He left the shop for the field, where he became an expert at nondestructive, nonchemical methods of capture. He traveled to the Philippines and was appalled by the cyanide cycle he observed there.

In 1985—with Peter Rubec, a Canadian fisheries biologist, and Vaughan Pratt, an American wildlife veterinarian—Robinson began the International Marinelife Alliance. While Pratt and Rubec—joined by Don E. McAllister of Canada's National Museum of Natural Sciences—raised funds, Robinson converted cyanide fishermen at every opportunity, retraining them in net techniques that spared the coral. IMA had no help from the Marcos government, and for the first year of its existence the going was slow for the outfit.

In 1986, with People Power, the revolution, and Corazon Aquino, there came a dramatic change. President Aquino declared a "National Consciousness Week Against Destructive Fishing." She established the Anti-Illegal Fishing Task Force, in which the Coast Guard, Navy, Bureau of Fisheries, and Ministry of Agriculture collaborate to enforce laws against fishing with cyanide and dynamite. Several hundred cyanide distributors and fish dynamiters have been arrested to date. IMA has become a quasi-official organization in the Philippine government. In the first year of the new era, Robinson retrained more than 200 cyanide fishermen. He estimates he has around 2,000 to go.

Edgardo Gomez, founder and director of the Bolinao Marine Laboratory, is himself—in his example, as much as his work—a promising development in the Philippines. Gomez has the very finest of credentials for a marine biologist, a doctorate from Scripps. Third World scholars who earn PhDs from the best American institutions generally find any number of reasons not to go home again. Gomez did go home. No sort of infrastructure awaited him. His first office was a single bare room. His first act was to get a telephone book to slip under the phone, so the place would have something like furniture. Gomez founded Bolinao Marine Lab so that he would *have* a lab; so that young Filipino marine scientists would not be greeted as he had been. He gave them a reason to come home.

Edgardo Gomez is tall for a Filipino. He has more Spanish ancestry in his features than is common among his countrymen. He wears a goatee and gold-rimmed bifocals, and his hair is showing its first gray. But after a few beers, in talking about his lab, his face will light up in boyish pleasure at the lab's accomplishments. Nine scholars are now working under him at Bolinao.

Last summer I interviewed Gomez in the company of Helen Yap, one of those scholars. If she had a single message to leave with my readers, I asked her, what would it be? She considered that, then said I should call attention to the problem of commercial shelling in the Philippines. "Tell Americans not to buy tropical shells," she said. When I asked the same question of Gomez, Yap leaned close to his ear. *"Tell Americans not to buy tropical shells,"* she stage-whispered. Grinning, Gomez dutifully repeated: "Tell Americans not to buy tropical shells."

Throughout our talk, Gomez was ever the cheerful optimist, Helen Yap the cheerful pessimist. I asked Gomez, among other things, if all the political turmoil of recent Philippine history had not been distracting.

"People have an exaggerated idea of what it's like," he said. "Never, through any of these troubles, did I have to miss a single day of work at the lab."

From what I understood, I said to Gomez, the Philippines were the best and worst. There were many devastated reefs in his islands, but among those undisturbed were some of the loveliest reefs in the world.

"Oh yes," Gomez answered. "There are seven thousand reefs in the Philippines. They can't blast all of them."

"Just wait," said Helen Yap.

VI
WILD PLANTS AND MAN

LILIES OF THE RAINBOW

PHOTOGRAPHY BY CHUCK DRESNER

*Previous pages: Nym-
phaea 'Albert Greenberg'*

*Nymphaea 'Antares'
(below)*

In July and August the water lily ponds justly
occupy center stage at Missouri Botanical
Garden in St. Louis. They are the legacy of
George Pring, a horticulturist trained at Kew
Gardens in England who came to America in
1906. Beginning with six kinds of wild water
lilies from Africa—species with modest blossoms of either blue or yellow—Pring crossed
and recrossed the plants to develop flowers of
greater size and varied, intense colors. These
are but a sample of the lilies of the rainbow.

Nymphaea 'Alice Tricker'

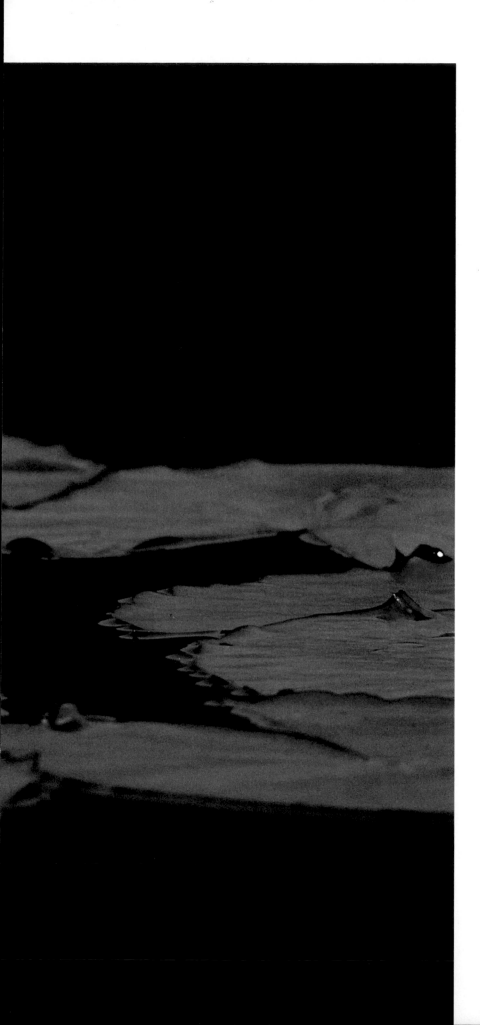

Nymphaea 'Director
George T. Moore'

Nymphaea 'Evelyn Randig'

Pincushion moss (Leucobryum glaucum)

DON'T LOOK DOWN ON THE HUMBLE MOSS

TEXT BY EDWARD R. RICCIUTI · PHOTOGRAPHY BY LARRY WEST

They are, in evolutionary terms, humble plants, without flowers or true roots. Their leaves are usually but one cell thick. In a literal sense, too, they are lowly. Some stand less than a millimeter high. Even the giants among the fifteen thousand species of mosses hardly reach above the ankle. If moss plants did not grow in clumps and mats, they would go unnoticed.

Even so, few people examine mosses closely, a shame. Mosses are like gorgeous, complex tapestries, as intricately patterned as any woven in Tabriz or Isfahan. The leaves of star moss grow in rosettes at the tip of stems. Other mosses are feathery or fernlike in appearance, while pincushion moss grows in dense, round clumps. Its thick, fleshy leaves give it a spongy feel. Flapper moss's lush tufts are green and touched with red. The red tinge looks like lipstick, which gave this plant its name, evocative of red-lipped ladies of the Roaring Twenties.

Most mosses prefer damp, shady places. The reason more moss grows on a tree's north side is that it is usually more shaded and moist. Apron moss is common on tree bark, as well as boulders. White-tipped moss favors rocky cliffs, while cascade moss grows in and along swift mountain streams, and sphagnum in bogs.

Mosses are tough. Neither summer's heat nor winter's cold conquers them. They are among the first plants to colonize barren areas, bringing new life to places scorched by forest fire, or anchoring by hairlike rhizomes on stark rock.

The reproduction of mosses have long fascinated scientists. Two-tailed sperm cells develop within a clublike male organ, the egg within a microscopic, flask-shaped cup. When the moss is wet, the male sex organ absorbs water and bursts, ejecting the sperm.

The sperm is mobile, but seems to rely on passive transfer to the vicinity of the female organ. Reduced surface tension in the sheet of water on the plant may slide the sperm toward its destination. Raindrops or an insect may carry it there. As the sperm arrives, the cap covering the female flask bursts, opening a canal to the egg. Possibly attracted by sugar in the flask, the sperm squeezes through the canal and fertilizes the egg.

After fertilization, a sporophyte begins to grow in the flask. It develops into a lidded capsule on a stalk, holding spores that will produce new moss plants. As the capsule grows, the flask around it stretches, the bottom part falls off, and the upper caps the lid until the capsule matures. On the Indian brave moss, a fragment of the flask tissue re-

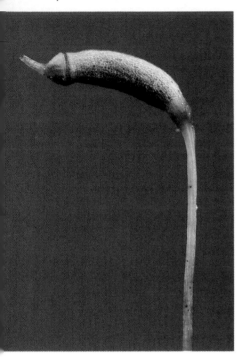

apper moss (Mnium
inulosum)

Indian brave moss
(Timmia megapolitana)

Pipe-cleaner moss
(Hypnum curvifolium)

mains and juts above the capsule, like a war-rior's feather.

Mosses release spores only in dry, breezy weather, when they have the best chance to disperse. The lid of typical moss spore cap-sules is ringed by flexible teeth that bend in when damp, shutting it tightly.

Sphagnum moss spore capsules operate differently. Tissues in the capsule wall absorb water, so swell when damp and shrink when dry. Shrinking creates pressure that blows off the lid, and the spores explode into the air. The "pop" of the minuscule blast is faintly audible.

After the spores settle, they divide into new moss plants. As it grows, moss reveals another aspect of its toughness. Slowly, but inexorably, moss destroys rock, loosening it into minute particles. This process of de-struction can open the door for new plant life. The rock particles and decaying moss leaves create soil, in which other plants, even small trees, can root. Where lowly moss once grew, trees may rise toward the sky.

Pincushion moss
(Leucobryum glaucum)

Bunchberry in Knight's-plume moss (Hypnum crista-castrensis)

Sphagnum moss (Sphagnum sp.)

Star moss (Mnium punctatum)

Apron moss (Anomodon sp.)

White-tipped moss (Hedwigia ciliata)

Wood frog on haircap moss (Polytrichum commune)

Cascade moss (Hygrohypnum sp.)

UNDERACHIEVER OF THE PLANT WORLD

TEXT BY DAVID M. SCHWARTZ • PHOTOGRAPHY BY DWIGHT R. KUHN

In his Salt Lake City office, agronomist Jess Martineau has an old black-and-white photograph of Henry Ford proudly thumping his latest model coupé—with an ax. The picture is not an ad for the car. It's a demonstration of what Ford, and the world, got for the millions he invested in an unknown crop from China. The automobile body, Ford's suit, and all the other things in the picture except the ax were made from soybeans.

If things had gone the way Martineau hoped, there might have been another picture in his office at NPI, the world's largest plant biotech firm, formerly called Native Plants, Inc. It would be a picture, perhaps, of two people at dinner. The meat and vegetables on the table, the wine, the wax and wick of the candles, the paint on the walls and stuffing in the chairs, the paper of the menu, even the tableware and the diners' clothing—all of it would have come from milkweed, that well-known but little-exploited colonizer of roadsides and fallow ground. (The meat, you ask? Well, the livestock would have foraged on milkweed hay and eaten milkweed seed meal; then the medallions would have been sautéed in polyunsaturated milkweed oil.)

That no such picture exists can't be blamed on Martineau. He has spent most of this decade pursuing its fruition. Milkweed, rampant plant that it is, can't be faulted either. It was up to the task. But economic forces more potent than either Martineau or milkweed refused to cooperate.

Collectively, the 107 North American species of *Asclepias,* a worldwide genus of plants, were supposed to have been the next soybean, or better. The list of possible milkweed products and by-products is even longer than that for soybeans. True, admitted the enthusiasts of yesteryear, the milky sap contains enough cardiac glycosides to kill a cow, but they can be detoxified; once that's done, you've got a first-class livestock feed. And the seed oil, nutritionally similar to soybean oil, can be sold for kitchen use.

But food and feed are just the beginning. Indigenous peoples of at least two continents have made rope and textiles from the stem fibers, said milkweed boosters; maybe we can even turn them into paper pulp.

In case anyone was yet to be convinced, *Asclepias* turned up on the list of plants whose extracts might substitute for fossil fuels. The pundits declared that with the right technology they could separate milkweed's chemical components and extract the hydrocarbons, tapping the solar energy trapped inside the plants immediately rather than waiting for natural decomposition. The hydrocarbons have myriad other uses: Thomas Edison demonstrated that the white latex could be made into natural rubber; and then there are plastics, pharmaceuticals, industrial lubricants, meat tenderizers, chewing gum, sugars, pectin . . . Once tamed, the argument went, milkweed will be just the ticket for beleaguered American agriculture, especially in the semiarid western Great Plains where the showy milkweed, *Asclepias speciosa,* is right at home. Let the Ogallala Aquifer run dry; these little guys don't need irrigation. Just plant the seeds and reap the weeds.

And so, a vision emerged of milkweed monocultures spreading out in every bioclimatic zone. Energy plantations across the land. Funded by the Departments of Agriculture and Energy along with fiber and fuel companies, Jess Martineau and friends went to work. Six hundred sugar beet and soybean acres in Nebraska were turned over to a plant that most farmers had grown up trying to eradicate. Their vocabulary was slow to accommodate its newly elevated status. "The weeds outgrew the weeds," said David Haun, one of the contractors, explaining why his stands were slow to take. But Martineau was undaunted. "Eventually, we figured out how to break dormancy on the seed, we learned how to plant it, we found out how to get rid of the weeds, we even worked out a way to harvest it mechanically and put it through a ginning apparatus." He projected that 100,000 acres would be planted with milkweed by 1995.

Then oil prices plummeted, and a new phrase began to fleck the discussion of milk-

Thomas Edison made rubber from the gummy sap of common milkweed (Asclepias syriaca); *milkweed flowers at left.*

Milkweed floss pinch-hit for kapok to fill Navy life preservers during World War II, and schoolchildren gathered 25 million pounds of pods. An onion sack filled with dried pods weighed only four pounds.

weed crop development: "economic feasibility." That was something milkweed, despite its manifold promise, would not have until the price of crude reached somewhere around $60 a barrel. Although a major fiber company is reportedly interested in using milkweed floss, most research funding for *Asclepias* evaporated like a gasoline spill on hot Nebraska tarmac. In 1986 Standard Oil spent almost a half-million dollars on milkweed.

Like Martineau and Price, phytochemist Robert Adams spent several years milking milkweed for all it was worth, which turned out to be quite a bit but not quite enough. After determining that fuels extracted from the plants were simply not competitive, Adams, now director of Baylor University's Center for the Study of Famine and Agricultural Alternatives, turned toward other uses. "The waxes were suitable for high-temperature industrial lubricants," he says, "but they were equivalent to what was already on the market. So, we looked at the stem fibers and found them comparable to softwood pulp fibers in common use—just comparable. The plants yield a livestock feed with the same protein content as alfalfa, but detoxifying it can get expensive. Of course, the bioactive compounds have pharmaceutical potential, but there's about zero interest right now in

drugs derived from plants. The mentality is that we can synthesize anything."

That's sober language from a man who, in the heady days of 1983, authored a hugely optimistic report on milkweed utilization for the congressional Office of Technology Assessment. "What we've found since then is that if something is as good as what's already available, nobody's interested. They say it's not economically feasible. It's got to be five or six times, maybe ten times, better. If it's native while something else has to be imported, if it's a renewable source of hydrocarbons while something else is nonrenewable, if it can grow on marginal land while something else needs prime soil—none of that matters."

In a voice betraying disappointment, he adds, "Milkweed is still a very, very interesting plant with great potential, but it takes about fifty years to introduce a new crop in this country, and nobody's got a vision that extends that far." Then, portentously, sotto voce: "Yet, we're importing more oil now than ever before."

If milkweed optimism has withered on the stalk, it will likely leaf out again, for like the plant itself, human interest in it seems perennial. Time and again it has aroused a flurry of excitement; time and again something else has proved more effective, more

practical, more marketable, more—there's that phrase again—economically feasible. Time and again milkweed has shown itself to be the underachiever of the plant world.

Tracking the outcome of its swerves toward glory is like plotting a course through a town of dead-end streets. Old newspapers and trade journals are rife with chest-beating references to tantalizing new patents and upstart endeavors. But, like the predictions of a tabloid prophet, the published accounts look in only one direction. Rarely do they report the past, presumably because no news is better than bad news.

In 1814 the New York Society for the Promotion of Useful Arts reported that the common milkweed, *Asclepias syriaca,* although abundant, was never utilized in New York State. To illustrate the wasted potential, the society pointed out that the French employed milkweed in the manufacture of "cloth and velvets more lustrous than silk." Subsequently, several forays were made into the cultivation of the swamp milkweed, *A. incarnata,* and by the 20th Century an American textile scientist named Sydney Smith Boyce was publishing papers on a new fine-art fabric he called "ozone fiber." Cheaper than cotton or silk, it was said to combine the best qualities of both.

The fervor spread back across the Atlantic.

In 1928 a fledgling English company announced the development of a miracle fiber, "artificial cotton," the result of a secret chemical process. But within two years, the English Artificial Cotton Production and Marketing Corporation had gone out of business without even beginning commercial production. It was to be resurrected, in spirit, ten years later by a company formed to market yet another "new" fiber, "cotine." Like ozone and artificial cotton, cotine was a product of milkweed stem fiber, and it too died with nary an epitaph in the literature.

Thomas Edison—using the gummy sap of common milkweed—was one of the early champions of milkweed latex as a rubber source, but eventually he abandoned the idea of commercial production. In the early 1940s, Douglas Aircraft Company tested milkweed rubber as a fireproof fuel-tank liner in military aircraft, with heartening results reported in *Popular Mechanics.* Cultivation, the magazine announced, would "produce enough rubber in two years to furnish all domestic needs for both civilian and military aviation." Needless to say, it never happened. Investigators took another look in the 1980s, and they found milkweed rubber impressive in every respect except one—it couldn't be processed in the existing facilities designed to accommodate the higher-

Overleaf: A harvest of milkweed edibles: (clockwise) flower buds, shoots, young seed pods, and tender leaves.

173

Aphids sucking juice from milkweed leaf

A jumping spider with a deer fly

Plume moth near its pupal skin

LIFE IN A MILKWEED JUNGLE

Red milkweed beetle on flowers

Milkweed bugs feeding on maturing seeds

Camouflaged crab spider with honeybee

Casebearer on milkweed leaf

Four or five days after a monarch butterfly deposits a tiny egg on a milkweed leaf, the caterpillar chews its way through the shell (center). During its two-week larval life, a growing caterpillar will shed its skin four times (below). Monarch caterpillars browse exclusively on milkweed plants, and the bitter sap gives them a foul taste that will deter predators. Moreover, the chemicals remain in the insect after metamorphosis, and any bird making a meal of a monarch butterfly will not repeat the mistake.

molecular-weight rubber of the Malaysian *Hevea* tree.

Only once—and it took a world war—did milkweed ascend to the elevated realm of economic consequence. When the Japanese seized the Dutch East Indies in 1942, the United States had to find an alternative to kapok, the cottony seed fiber found in the outsized pods of *Ceiba pentandra*, the silk-cotton tree. Although native to the American tropics, hundred-foot *Ceiba* trees had long been cultivated on Java, where enormous plantations supplied the world with kapok for upholstery and other uses. Lightweight, moisture-resistant, and buoyant, it was the perfect filler for life preservers, and without a supply to stuff sailors' "Mae West" vests, the Navy feared there would soon be a mass descent upon Davy Jones' locker.

A pinch-hitter was found in milkweed. "Pick a weed, save a life!" implored the Department of Agriculture at the Navy's behest. Outfitted with empty onion sacks, armies of schoolchildren and Scout troops fanned out across the roadsides and fallow fields of twenty-six states. Their mission: to collect ripe milkweed pods and ship them to a government-financed processing plant in Petoskey, Michigan, where the pods and seeds would be separated from the flossy seed hairs. Waxy on the outside and hollow within, each thread of milkweed floss was an air-enclosing tube that closely resembled kapok: Twenty-six ounces of it could keep a 150-pound man afloat in saltwater for forty-eight hours.

And pick is what the children did. Whether motivated more by patriotism or the incentive of twenty cents a bag it is impossible to say, but during the last two years of the war they collected 25 million pounds of pods, enough, when dried and ginned, to fill 1.2 million life vests with floss. For once an achiever, milkweed saved many an Allied sailor from a watery grave. But when the war was over, the milkweed floss program sank and drowned: The cost of processing floss in Michigan was seventy-five cents a pound, while a pound of kapok could be imported for ten cents.

Economic unfeasibility is nothing new to this plant.

I did not need a war to appreciate *Asclepias*. Nor do I need hydrocarbons, textiles, pharmaceuticals, or any other ulterior motive. I am quite happy to accept milkweed on its own terms. After all, it is the plant that outscored all others on the Gee Whiz scale.

Professor Bill Keeton never knew it, but he created the Gee Whiz scale. In the late 1960s, his Biology 101 lectures at Cornell, so

flush with hard principles and processes, were also garnished with eyebrow-raising examples of nature's more astonishing adaptations—and his were the eyebrows that rose the most. To a small circle of my fellow freshmen, the dance of the honeybees, the distinctive mate-identification flash patterns of courting fireflies (and those *femmes fatales* who imitated other species' mating signals to attract—and eat—them), the orientation of homing pigeons by the Earth's magnetic field when celestial cues were obscured by clouds—these and a thousand other examples were fodder for the subdiscipline that we

dubbed "Gee Whiz Biology." The elegance of each vignette, which usually corresponded directly with the lift in Doc Keeton's eyebrows, was measured on the Gee Whiz scale, whose one-to-ten ratings were awarded by consensus over lunch.

Being zoologically inclined, most of us were unlikely to afford anything over a 7 or 8 to a mere plant—until we met the milkweed. Here was the paradigm of botanical Gee Whiz.

For starters, it was a gorgeous thing. Its umbels of creamy pink and lavender blossoms add color to even the least savory road-

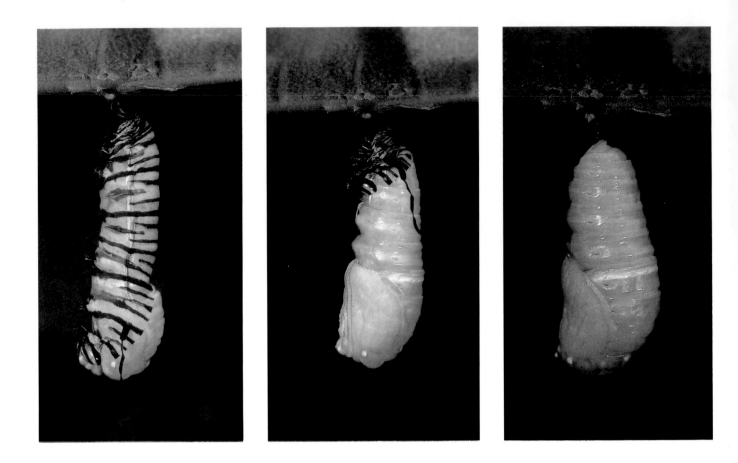

Securing itself to the underside of a milkweed leaf, a fully grown monarch caterpillar molts its larval skin for the last time and proceeds to form a chrysalis around its body.

sides in midsummer, and its warty pods dehisce to release silken parachutes of floss that ride shafts of light on backlit autumn afternoons. Further, if boiled in several changes of water (as prescribed by Euell Gibbons, one of the patron saints of Gee Whiz Biology), young shoots, early leaves, unopened buds, and immature pods can be eaten, a trait bound to win the plant friends among perpetually hungry—and, of course, hard up—college students. Then there was the relationship of milkweeds to monarch and viceroy butterflies, surely one of nature's most exquisite machinations.

Unlike most herbivores, which shun milkweed, monarch caterpillars feed exclusively on *Asclepias.* They steep their tissues in the plant's bitter sap, which transfers to the browsers the protection that comes from tasting foul. The milkweed's chemicals remain in the insect's body even after metamorphosis. To the bird that mistakes a monarch butterfly for dinner, the meal becomes a wrenching, retching memory. But the blundering aggressor quickly learns its lesson, and from that moment on will avoid any potential prey with the monarch's distinctive orange-and-black coloration.

Now consider the viceroy. This butterfly, not a milkweed feeder, could be an in-

sectivore's delight—but viceroys are deadringers for monarchs. Consequently, no well-educated blue jay considers a viceroy fit to eat. The protection that a palatable species gains by mimicking a distasteful one is so effective that the strategy has cropped up in many corners of the animal kingdom. First described in 1861 by the English naturalist H. W. Bates, who spent eleven years studying butterflies in Brazil, this kind of defense has come to be called Batesian mimicry. The classic example remains that of the viceroys and monarchs, whose resemblance is based ultimately on milkweeds.

There was a good story, and of course it earned high marks from the Gee Whiz evaluators; but not until we peered down the binocular barrels of a dissecting microscope did the wonders of milkweed really come alive. The little flowers were transformed from mere splashes of color to baffling puzzles with a remarkable solution.

Charles Darwin, who devoted an entire book to the pollination of orchids, had little to say about milkweed flowers, even though their unique structures and bizarre pollination confounded botanists for more than two hundred years. To us in Bio 101, with the standard "Parts of a Flower" diagram still fresh in mind, nothing about the milkweed

flower made any sense at all until, coaxed by our instructor, the blossoms stubbornly yielded their secrets.

To be sure, the expected parts are all there, but none looks the way the chart says it's supposed to. Sepals are small and folded out of sight behind recurved petals that point down the stem. The showiest parts of the flower, five fleshy, nectar-filled flagons called "hoods," are actually outgrowths of highly modified stamens. Normally, stamens consist of threadlike filaments topped by an enlarged anther, but in the milkweed the anthers and the style (the pistil's slender stalk) are fused into a central column. Here's where things get really peculiar: The column is divided by five vertical slits, wide at the bottom and narrowing toward the top, where they terminate in a small black dot called a corpusculum.

And so the drama begins. Arrives an insect, let us say a bumblebee. Drawn by a profusion of nectar, the bee attempts to anchor itself on the smooth cylinder. Not an easy task, it finds, made even less so by incurving "horns" that arise from the middle of each hood. (No botanist has yet ascribed a definitive function to these crescent-shaped projections, but several have speculated that their purpose is to make it even more diffi-

cult for the visitor to alight.) Awkwardly pumping its feet—as though it were on snowshoes, wrote Edwin Way Teale—the unbalanced insect may gain its only foothold in one of the column's five crevices. Which is hardly a coincidence.

When it is full of nectar and tries to decamp, the insect suddenly finds its tarsus snared by nature's version of a leg-hold trap. The corpusculum, it turns out, is really a clasp at the apex of a wishbone-shaped structure called a "translator," the rest of which is hidden from view inside the column. If the surfeited insect is too small or weak to dislodge its leg it will meet a lingering death as prisoner of the bloom. Many a fly and honeybee have perished in this way, and many others have managed to escape with only five appendages. But a bumblebee can usually muster enough strength to pull free. Still, it must pay a price for its refreshment, and at this point the purpose of all this tomfoolery becomes clear: With the extricated leg comes the flower's translator, torn loose from its internal mooring, and hanging from each translator arm is a waxy sac of pollen. (By mimicking the action of a bee's leg with a needle, anyone can—and, of course, we did—remove the translator and its pollinia from a milkweed flower.)

Metamorphosis from caterpillar to butterfly takes about two weeks, the adult monarch finally emerging from a translucent chrysalis shell to unfold and dry its wings, then fly away.

A GLORIOUS TRAP

Lured by an abundance of sweet nectar in the milkweed's remarkable flower, a honey-bee finds its only foothold in one of five vertical slits separating the showy "hoods." Once surfeited, the bee discovers that its tarsus has been snared by nature's own leg-hold trap. In the insect's struggle for freedom, waxy sacs of pollen become wrapped around its leg—and are carried to another flower, completing pollination.

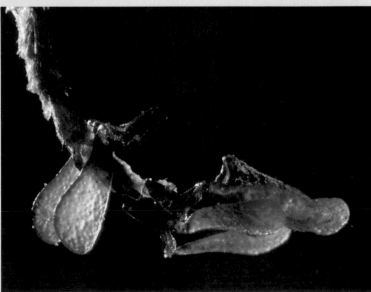

Autumn's seeds, sprung from dry pods and windborne on flossy parachutes, launch spring's new generation of milkweed plants.

on another flower? Perhaps, conjectured Teale, the improbability of pollination explained the small number of pods on his hillside, compared with an earlier profusion of flowers. He counted only thirty-two pods ripening where some 10,000 milkweed flowers had bloomed.

But no, says Susan Stone Bookman, whose close observations of milkweeds at Washington State University determined that the pollinators did their job well—so well, in fact, that the plants would arch to the ground if all the pollinated flowers bore fruit. Instead, Bookman found that most of the flowers on any one plant aborted their pods. She wondered: Do they abort randomly or in some consistent fashion? Does the quality of the pollen have any effect?

Playing pollinator herself, Bookman tested strains of pollen from many different plants. When she pollinated stingily, introducing pollinia to only a few flowers on a plant, all produced ripe pods. Evidently, the pollen strains were viable. But when she offered the same mix of pollens in great abundance, most of it failed to result in fruit. A pattern emerged: In producing a relatively small number of pods, some pollens were being accepted while the majority were consistently rejected.

"The plants actually *selected* which pollen to accept and which to reject," says Bookman. "You could tell just from the looks of the seeds that some were superior to others. What the flowers were selecting was the pollen that produced the most viable seeds and presumably the most vigorous plants." Like female animals who choose a mate based on his fitness, milkweed plants somehow reject the losers and single out the pollen with the most promising male genes.

Now we're talking *serious* Gee Whiz. I can see Doc Keeton's eyebrows on the rise.

Off flies the insect, shaking its encumbrance along the way—another act that serves the flower's purpose by rotating the pollen sacs 90 degrees. When our clumsy courier lands again, the pollinia face in just the right direction to fit into one of the stigmatic slits in the new flower's column. If that happens, pollination is complete.

This chain of events may seem highly improbable. How many bees and butterflies can be expected to sink a leg into such a minuscule crevice—and then do it all over again

VII
SPECIAL PLACES

THE SWAMP

TEXT BY DANIEL JACK CHASAN

The swamp began a little east of our house. Across the gravel road and through the trees the ground grew softer, the vegetation changed, and after a few more steps, when I walked there after school or on the weekends or any day in the summer, I was in a different world.

It was not, I'm sure, a place of great biological significance (no rare or endangered or esthetically remarkable species lived there, as far as I know), and it was hardly the forest primeval. There were a few big trees in the vicinity—the oak that grew outside our living room window must have stood there for centuries—but the scrubby hardwoods in the swamp were third growth at best. The water in their midst was shallow, deep enough to get a boy's feet thoroughly soaked but little more than a web of perpetual puddles. Pale grass rose from the water in shaggy clumps. I traveled in a series of long, careful steps and short, anxious leaps from clump to clump. Near the far edge of the swamp, friends of mine later trapped muskrats and mink, but the only wild animal I ever saw there was a woodchuck.

At the near edge of the swamp, where the ground was damp but not squishy, wildflowers grew. When I was very young, probably eight or nine, I decided to transplant some of those flowers. I dug them up with a trowel, carried them in I don't remember what, and planted them in the bleak space along the wall of our garage. I didn't know anything about transplanting, and I'm sure I shouldn't have been moving wild plants around anyway, but somehow it worked: The flowers bloomed there every spring until my parents sold the house, after I had graduated from college. For all I know, they still bloom there every spring. I sometimes wonder.

But the flowers weren't the main attraction for me. The main attraction was the swamp itself. Occasionally, I took a friend there, but usually I went alone or with a dog. The swamp may not have been especially wild or remote, but it was unlike any other place I knew, and it was somehow *complete:* Within it, I couldn't see or hear anything outside, wasn't aware of anything beyond the trees.

Sometimes there must have been a good deal of fantasy involved. Certainly I liked to think I was accomplishing an heroic feat as I leaped from one dry clump of grass to another, and I think there may have been some not entirely subliminal echoes of Humphrey Bogart making his way through the jungle in *The African Queen.*

Even without the fantasy, I had the privacy, the enclosure, the sense of a different world. I knew I could spend all afternoon there without meeting anyone else. I also knew or suspected or at least hoped that the swamp had its secrets: events and maybe places that I never saw. When the dogs went there without me, I wished there were some way of fastening little movie cameras to their backs, so I could see where they went and what they did when I wasn't along. I envisioned Disney epics of claw and fang taking place somewhat below knee height, but I never saw any sign of them. What I did see, all alone, was a stream, far back, that flowed smoothly under banks of arching trees. I can still remember walking southeast past a couple of fallen trees and coming on the dull gray-green surface of the water. The trouble is, I'm not sure the stream existed outside my dreams. I wasn't sure even then. I knew I had seen it, more than once, but I never knew where.

Other places were easier to find, and I gave some of them special names, which must have come from books I read at the time. One large open space was "The King's Meadows."

I remember what a shock it was when The King's Meadows was obliterated by a wide swath cut through the heart of the swamp for a high-tension powerline. That was the beginning of the end. The place where the wildflowers grew was buried under the asphalt of a small new road. Finally, in exchange for some kind of tax break, the whole closer portion of the swamp was given to the township in which we lived as the site for a new town hall. It was a miserable building site; but after all the trees were cut and Lord knows how many loads of fill were dumped—the fill kept sinking, much to my delight, but the trucks kept bringing more—it wasn't a swamp anymore. It was a low, ugly, modern office building with plastic-paneled walls and a large parking lot. (The transformation was not abrupt, of course;

there was a prolonged intermediate stage of broken trees and freshly bulldozed dirt.)

For all practical purposes, I think that was the end of the swamp. In terms of square feet, this may or may not have been true; but in my mind at least, all that survived were remnants. By now, even those remnants probably have been buried under fill and suburban housing. Even if they have not, and even if I didn't now live a continent away, I probably wouldn't go there again. It is all a very remote memory.

At the time, it wasn't remote at all. When I was in ninth grade—classes began in September 1957, only days before the U.S.S.R. put the first satellite into orbit—technological progress was exalted with desperate intensity, but I wrote an essay against progress. I included some borrowed diatribes against modern art and modern jazz (I had read a book by someone who believed that every-

thing past Benny Goodman was sheer decadence), but they were mainly window dressing. What I started with, and what I cared about, was the building of that powerline through the swamp.

Even then, I realized that I was probably the only person in the world who had cared about the swamp, and that presumably the powerline—like the road and town hall—had been built to serve some greater good. Realizing that didn't change the way I felt, though, and hasn't kept me from reacting negatively to that kind of "progress" ever since. I am not deaf to the arguments in favor of building. I may even agree with them. Often, I do. But my reaction, my reflex, is always contrary. I sometimes wonder if at that level—the level of instinctive response—when I see freshly broken trees and flayed earth, I still see *them* trying to bulldoze their way through *my* swamp.

THAT SPECIAL THIRST

TEXT BY PAUL QUINNETT

•

PAINTING BY FRANCIS GOLDEN

From the end of the road you can see where the old trail leads up from the river and cuts across the side of the draw and disappears into the alder. "The Forest Service stopped the trail work several years back," a local had told us, "so the going won't be easy. But there's a saddle up there that's never been logged. Too hard to get to. Some of that country is steeper than a cow's face."

Hard to get to was okay with me. Going where others can't or won't is what I had in mind. But steeper than a *cow's face*?

"What do you think?" I asked my middle son, shutting off the car. "Are you up for it?"

Being a typically garrulous fifteen-year-old, he glanced at the mountain and shrugged his shoulders.

"Then let's hit it," I said. "If we get into them, believe me, it'll be worth the effort."

We were five hours on the road getting there. The weather had been perfect, and we'd made good time. We'd seen some deer from the highway, and an osprey; crossing the Idaho panhandle we'd seen a moose standing in a slough by the Pack River. But driving through most of western Montana you have to look straight ahead not to have your heart broken—that is if you're the sort of person who sees something other than board feet and profit margins when you pass a stand of timber. The clearcuts do it to you. Every which way you look, you can see them: forests sheared flush to the ground, ridges and valleys scarred with access roads and festooned with power poles. If you didn't know better, you'd think we'd hired a bunch of punk rockers to redesign our wild country.

But we hadn't come to grieve the clearcuts or the powerlines, the timber roads or the heavy metals leaching into mountain streams from the mining operations. You can do all that kind of grief work in the comfort of your living room. No, we had come to do a bit of

fishing and to climb to a high place, to be in the black timber, the old-growth stuff, and maybe see an elk or two.

"How far up?" my son asked.

"Halfway at least. Maybe less. We've got all day."

(I laid the "all day" line as foundation for later on when, as senior hiker, I might need to pause to study some distant peak or examine a mushroom, as in, "Hey, take it easy. We've got all day.")

"Are you sure about the elk?" the boy asked.

"It's a big mountain," I said, "but I think we'll find them. There are only so many places they can go on a day like today."

July. Hot. Humid. The sun is up early and long now, beating hard on the south-facing slopes. Mosquitoes are thick in the high grasses along the river, and trout are rising from their lies to take breakfast. We are glad to start up and away from the insects and the whine of truck engines along the highway. The downdraft of cool air is in our face. We build a quick heat, and the jackets come off.

On the lower reaches the track leads up through second-growth timber and you can see the old skid-trails where the Cats cut in and the logs went down by saw and chain to river and market. The stumps are there. You can kneel and age them, guess the cutting year, find your birth year, see the wet years and the dry ones, and wonder at the whirls in the heartwood. If you close your eyes and try to imagine, it is still hard to see how it must have been here once, before the big, easy trees were felled.

Crossing a small rivulet, we pause where a spring oozes from the base of a vertical rise of stone. Taking turns, we kneel and drink.

"We could be fishing," the boy says.

"We will. This evening."

The boy wasn't sure about climbing a mountain in the middle of a fishing trip to maybe see an elk, with emphasis on the maybe. But I had insisted. I have been in the old-growth many times, and once you have gone there it is difficult not to think about the black trees and cool places—especially when you are hot and thirsty and the city noise is in your ears and your eyes water from something called suspended particulates and you know that even if you step into an air-conditioned lounge and order something wet poured into a tall glass of chipped ice you will not quench that special thirst. Only in places where people don't go can you do that—in the hard-to-get-to places, places where the elk bed.

Gone back to the wild, the trail begins to peter out. Even the animals no longer use it.

Before us in the cleavage of the mountain the alder branches arch, lock up one to another, and make the going impossible. Pushing upward, we hit a creek large enough to make noise, and work above yew trees and vine maple in the bottom. If you stay on the side hills and above the tops of the cedars in the bottoms you will be where the deer go, and the walking, though never easy, is much better.

"Where's the trail?" asks the boy.

"Dunno."

"Why don't they keep them up anymore?"

"No money, they say. But they seem to have plenty for logging roads."

"Don't start on that," the boy says.

He knows me well.

An hour into the climb we begin to find elk spoor. It is bleached out and gray and crumbles easily between your fingers. The herd was here, but months ago. So close to the river, this is probably winter range. But at least we know we are on the same mountain with elk. There are a lot of elk in Montana, although they never seem to be quite where you'd like them to be. Still, in the heat of July, you can at least count on where they will *not* be. They will not be standing in wide-open parks enjoying the sunshine. They will not be near the riverbottoms or at the lower elevations. If there is a logging operation in one mountain valley, they will move to the next, or at least far enough away to get the ring of chainsaws out of their ears. If a heavily used timber road cuts through their range, they will cross it only if forced or driven. And generally they will not spend time on the ridges and peaks—that is the stuff of which movies are made.

"So, just exactly where are these elk?" asks the boy, as I call a halt to examine a stand of bear grass and pant that, after all, we have all day.

I pull the map from my day pack and spread it on the surface of a rock. Finding the saddle and the little basin above it, I point to a spot where three small, spring-fed streams come together in one of those green-tinted areas the cartographers use to indicate woods. "There. That's where I would be if I were an elk. Looks like another thousand feet and over to our right."

"How do you know they'll be there?" asks the boy.

I think to explain how it is I came to be such an expert elk-finder or how—if one can but read a map and knows how to find the old-growth and knows enough about animal behavior to know to what lengths a creature as intelligent as a wapiti will go to avoid contact with human beings—just about any beginner can go into most any elk habitat and walk right up to the local herd. But what I say is, "Years of experience, my boy. Years of experience." (It is very difficult these days for a father to gain credibility with a fifteen-year-old, so I can't let this opportunity slip by.)

We climb another hour. I try to keep my huffing and puffing to a minimum and remind myself of the old saying, "As he is now, I once was. As I am now, he will become." But, for some reason, waxing philosophical doesn't seem to make a cow's face any less steep or put any more air into my lungs.

We cross a large rockslide and head up into a stand of lodgepole pine that, from the map, looks to be along the lower edge of the saddle. We are nearly halfway up the side of the mountain. Here is grass as high as your calves. And the first serious game trails. Deer droppings. Bear scat. Dark, nearly black elk pellets that crush smoothly between your fingers and hang together with a certain freshness. We find the first beds: big ones, smelling of urine. A grouse flushes. The blood comes up.

There is no need for talking now. We move single-file up through the lodgepoles, angling toward our right. I insist on the lead, not because I know better where to go, but because I don't want us to blunder into them.

Suddenly, we are there. Over a scree of rock and set against a gentler slope above us the old-growth looms. Huge trunks rising. Douglas firs too big for two men to reach around. The stand is too tall to see over and too thick to see through. Inside the timber it is dark, shadowy, promising. And from below, with the breeze wafting toward us, we can *feel* the old-growth—cool and rich with the smell of wild animals. We move quickly across the scree.

A few steps inside the black timber we find heavy piles of elk droppings, the sort of stools left by unhurried animals. There are beds everywhere. We count six in one grouping. You can see the way they lay and, getting down to your knees, you can see what they can see when they are bedded. I show the boy a horn tree stripped of bark higher than a man can reach and spread my arms wide over my head to make the sign of a bull. He smiles. His eyes have a light in them. He too can sense the elk are near. We move upstream, our faces into the river of air pouring down the mountain.

The floor in the old-growth is a smooth carpet of needles, and the game trails cut deep enough to expose the soil. The trails run parallel to the mountain, slanting gently up or down. For short stretches, some are almost as wide as a city sidewalk. Even a man can go quietly in such a place.

I whisper to the boy that we are in luck with the wind, that if it doesn't change we should be in them soon. We crouch low, pick our steps, and move quietly upward. It is almost midday, and out on the scree you could feel the sun press against your skin and had to swat away the blackflies. But in here, in the old-growth, it is as if you are in another clime or country, a shaded realm where the air is cool and the ferns grow tall. I shiver as if taking a sudden chill, but I do not think it is because of the temperature change.

Some people do not believe it, but it is true: When the wind is right you can smell elk before you see them.

I stop. The boy stops behind me. I point to my nose and make a sniffing sound.

Perplexed, he cocks his head and whispers: "What?"

"Smell. You can smell them."

But it is too late. From the timber above us we hear a loud crack, nearly as loud as the crack of a small pistol. Excluding a man or range cattle or a spooked bear, only one animal will do that in this wild place. Unlike deer or coyotes or cats, elk don't care much for silent running. They don't need to.

"Elk!" I whisper.

I can see them now. Lying flat on the duff, I can look up through the timber and see their legs moving; a head here, a torso there, antlers twisting high far back in the herd, they are coming. I can see their rich brown fur flash in the columns of sunlight between the trees. There are many elk, maybe twenty of them. We can hear the soft *meows* of the calves and cows. They are headed right for us.

I do not like the word "walk" to describe how elk move. Amble, yes. Saunter, yes. Crash off when spooked, yes. But not walk. Walk is not magic enough. From afar, elk passing through the woods seem to float. These elk, the ones moving inexorably toward us, are drifting.

The boy is down behind a tree, I behind another. The herd will pass on either side. I don't know about the boy, but there is thunder in my chest.

For two minutes, maybe three, they are all around us, calling softly to one another. Hooves shuffle in the dry needles, raising dust. Their aroma fills the air. A pair of spike bulls shove each other. A cow noses her calf, pushing it ahead of her. Heads swing on thick necks. Twigs snap. The high, yellow-buff rumps bob through the black timber. They step, gliding, over logs as high as a man's thigh as if they are not lying there.

Grace. Power. Beauty. If there is a herd bull, I cannot see him. But a young bull raises his head sharply, as if something is amiss, and studies us. We remain frozen. We are down-wind, and he cannot smell us.

And then they are gone—drifting down and away from us in that noisy, *crack, pop, snap* way that elk have when they are moving unhurriedly through the understory of the old-growth. Finally a straying calf scents us. She starts, looks back, and then trots away to catch up with the herd.

I think to follow them, but know it is no good. The down-draft thermal will give us away. Soon the breezes will begin to shift and blow randomly through the early afternoon until, unless you are just dumb lucky, there is no getting close to this herd or any other. I turn to the boy.

"She looked me right in the eye!" he says. "I could have reached out and touched her! Really! I could have touched her!"

There is a good feeling where the thunder was.

"Let's go after them!"

I shake my head, but say that if he wants to he can try to stalk them once again. "I'll be right here, waiting for you," I say. "We've got all day." Then he is off, loping down through the timber.

I roll my jacket into a pillow and stretch out flat in the middle of a bed so that I can smell deeply of the elk that slept here. It is a wonderful bed: cool, smooth, dry under the canopy. I gaze up through the tall black timber to the high, bright Montana sky. For now, for this moment, for this day, the thirst is quenched.

192